WINTER
WARMERS

20 STYLISH KNITS TO KEEP YOU COZY

© Crea © Eaglemoss Ltd. 2019
1st Floor, Beaumont House,
Kensington Village,
Avonmore Rd,
London W14 8TS

ISBN 978-1-85875-605-9

Printed in China

Yarn care instructions
Hand wash only • Do not bleach
• Do not iron • Do not tumble dry
When washing the finished product follow
the manufacturer's washing instructions
found on the yarn bands.

WINTER
WARMERS

20 STYLISH KNITS TO KEEP YOU COZY

crea CRAFTS

CONTENTS

WELCOME!

Here at CreaCrafts we have really enjoyed putting together this selection of knits using the beautiful yarns in our collection. We hope you will enjoy our themes of a Winter Walk, being Cozy at Home, and Café Dining, each one was the inspiration for a mini collection of knits. But, of course, it is up to you to decide what you want to wear and when!

Whether you are a beginner or a pro-knitter, try the Cozy Cowl using the yarn supplied with the book—and we hope you will love making all our Winter Warmers. Have fun!

The Crea Team

YOUR CREA YARNS

Inspired by the natural tones in nature, each yarn type has been spun in a gorgeous range of soft, tactile textures. Here is your guide to the beautiful yarns used in this book:

GRISAILLE is a bouclé fashion yarn 1 oz. (25g)/ 44 yd. (40m) 100% polyester

PROVENANCE is a double knitting yarn 1 oz. (25g)/ 55 yd. (50m) 80% acrylic/20% wool

HARMONY is a double knitting yarn 1 oz. (25g)/71 yd. (65m) 100% acrylic

ANTIQUE is a bulky yarn 1 oz. (25g)/33 yd. (30m) 100% acrylic

SHADOW is a worsted-type yarn 1 oz. (25g)/55 yd. (50m) 60% acrylic/40% polyester

PARAGONE is a bulky yarn 1 oz. (25g)/60 yd. (55m) 98% acrylic/2% nylon

IMPASTO is a double knitting yarn 1 oz. (25g)/49 yd. (45m) 50% wool/50% acrylic

HAPTIC is a fluffy fashion yarn 1 oz. (25g)/44 yd. (40m) 50% acrylic/50% nylon

You can order all the yarns used in the book, in a range of gorgeous colors, from www.creacrafts.com

LET'S GET STARTED...

Here are just a few things to note so you can make the most of this book, such as how to read the patterns, where to find techniques and information, and your essential kit.

When choosing your project to knit, always look in the Materials box to find out what you need for each project. You can get started with your Cozy Cowl (page 12) right away, but if you want to order any other yarns, just go to www.creacrafts.com and follow the links to the online shop.

For each project, the color, quantity, and type of yarn needed to complete a project are listed first, followed by the knitting needle sizes—you will also find a crochet hook handy for some things—followed by any other materials needed to complete a project.

Garments may have sizes and figures in square brackets [ ] refer to the larger sizes where only one set of figures is given; this applies to all sizes, so check which one is right for you and make sure you have enough of the correct yarns.

Knitting patterns use abbreviations and you'll find that the instructions for making an item are always given in the same way. Read them carefully before you start and follow the stages in the order given. To get used to this type of text, see the inside back flap for the list of abbreviations you will need to follow throughout the Winter Warmers collection. If a pattern requires a special abbreviation, this will appear, in detail, in the pattern.

Gauge refers to the number of rows and stitches in a certain area, usually a 4 in. (10cm) square. If you get the gauge right, your project should end up the right size! Turn to page 85 to read more about how to get your gauge right.

Look out for our design bank features that show you how to customize your projects with pom-poms, tassels, buttons, and more. You'll also find essential techniques in Knitting Basics (see page 82), along with how to avoid mistakes, create cables, sew any seams perfectly—and more. You can also visit www.creacrafts.com for a selection of knitting and embellishing videos.

KNITTING KIT

Everyone's knitting kit is different, but some useful items are shown below—check your project first for what you need. It's also a treat to have a large enough bag for your yarns and needles, and a small case or container for your smaller items of equipment. Most items shown will be familiar, and you'll also want a row counter and some stitch markers (although a safety pin can also do the job). We have also included:

Circular needle: best for wide/heavy pieces of knitting.
Crochet hook: for picking up stitches and tassels.
Double-pointed needles: an option for small knits or using as a cable needle.
Needle gauge: especially good if it also has a ruler for measuring the gauge of your knitting.
Scissors: a small sharp pair for neat snips is great.
T-pins: useful for blocking garments.

WINTER WALKS

COZY COWL

This soft cowl will keep your neck warm when you're out and about on chilly days. It is made using simple knit and purl stitches while a bouclé yarn adds texture.

MATERIALS

- 4 x 1 oz. (25g) balls of Crea Grisaille in Moss, supplied with the book
- Pair of size 8 (5.0mm) knitting needles
- Tapestry needle
- Cardboard and scissors for tassels

Go to Knitting Basics pages 82–94 for advice on stitches, problem solving, and finishing your knits.

A series of fluffy tassels add a fun element to this cowl.

SIZE

31½ in. (80cm) in circumference x 13⅜ in. (34cm) long, excluding tassels.

GAUGE

12.5 sts and 23 rows = 4 in. (10cm) over st st.

ABBREVIATIONS

See back flap.

TO MAKE

Using size 8 (5.0mm) needles, cast on 100 sts loosely.
Beg with a k row, cont in st st until the work measures 13⅜ in. (34cm) from the beg, ending with a p row. Bind off loosely leaving a long yarn tail.

FINISHING

Join the seam for the center back (see Knitting Basics page 92). Make 8 tassels, each 2 in. (5cm) long (see Winter Walks Design Bank page 15). Sew the tassels around the bound-off edge, spacing them evenly, then trim the ends.

YOUR YARN

GRISAILLE YARN:

Along with the book, you have received 4 balls of Crea Grisaille in Moss, a bouclé yarn with a supersoft, fleecy effect that is ideal for making this fluffy cowl. It's easygoing in look and feel, and it is so light you can wear it indoors over sweaters, while the soft shade means it will partner well with both strong and subtle colors.

DESIGN BANK: **TASSELS**

Tassels add a special touch to fashion garments.
These simple embellishments are easy to make and add
a unique finishing touch to your projects.

Try out the amazing art of passementerie and create simple tassels to embellish your projects or ready-made items. Once you've got the hang of the basic technique, experiment making tassels with different threads and materials. Use plain or textured yarn, raffia, or narrow leather and suede strips, to make rustic tassels. Or combine silks, ribbons, and yarn to make luxurious, silky tassels.

Use scraps of yarn to make your tassels.

MAKING A BASIC TASSEL

Work in one color or use a combination of colors and fibers.

MATERIALS

- Yarn
- Cardboard
- Ruler
- Small sharp scissors
- Tapestry needle

1 *Cut the cardboard the required length of the tassel and about 2 in. (5cm) wide. Wrap the yarn around the cardboard to the required thickness. Thread a length of yarn onto a tapestry needle, slip it under the top loops and tie them loosely together—do not cut the ends as you will use them to attach the tassel.*

2 *Ease the loops off the cardboard. Cut a 31½ in. (80cm) length of yarn. Knot it around the tassel about one-third down from the top. Then wrap the end firmly around the tassel to cover the knot.*

3 *Thread the loose end of the yarn onto the tapestry needle and take it through the center of the tassel. Use sharp scissors to cut through the loops at the bottom of the tassel, then trim as required.*

PRETTY BOBBLE HAT

When you're staying outside, this bobble hat is the perfect way to keep your head warm. It's knitted in the garter stitch with just a few rows of simple shaping at the top.

MATERIALS

- 5 x 1 oz. (25g) balls of Crea Provenance in Albite
- 1 x 1 oz. (25g) ball of Crea Haptic in Filament
- Pair of size 6 (4.0mm) knitting needles
- Tapestry needle
- Pom-pom maker, 3½ in. (9cm) in diameter, or thin cardboard, pencil, pair of compasses and scissors
- Snap-on fasteners (see Designer's Tip on page 19)

SIZE

To fit an average size head. Length 9 in. (23cm), with brim turned back.

GAUGE

17 sts and 36 rows = 4 in. (10cm) over g st.

ABBREVIATIONS

See back flap.

TO MAKE

Using size 6 (4.0mm) needles and Albite, cast on 78 sts.
Work in g st (every row k) for 10 in. (25cm).

Shape top

Dec row 1: K1, *k2tog, k5, rep from * to the end of the row. 67 sts.
Next and every foll alt row: K to the end of the row.
Dec row 2: K1, *k2tog, k4, rep from * to the end of the row. 56 sts.
Dec row 3: K1, *k2tog, k3, rep from * to the end of the row. 45 sts.
Dec row 4: K1, *k2tog, k2, rep from * to the end of the row. 34 sts.
Dec row 5: K1, *k2tog, k1, rep from * to the end of the row. 23 sts.
Dec row 6: K1, *k2tog, rep from * to the end of the row. 12 sts.
Cut the yarn leaving a long yarn tail. Thread the cut end through the rem sts, draw up tightly, and secure the end.

A pom-pom is a quick and easy way to dress up this simple hat.

FINISHING

Use the yarn end to join the back seam (see Knitting Basics page 92), reversing the seam for 2 in. (5cm) for the brim. Turn back the brim.

Using Crea Haptic and the pom-pom maker (or cardboard circles), make a pom-pom (see Design Bank on right). Sew the pom-pom securely to the top of the hat. Alternatively, secure it with a snap-on fastener for a quick change—see Designer's Tip.

DESIGNER'S TIP

You could make interchangeable pom-poms for your hat! Just sew one half of a snap-on fastener to the top of the hat and the other half to the center of a pom-pom. Use a variety of yarns and colors to create different effects.

Make a selection of bobbles and change them to suit your mood (see Designer's Tip).

DESIGN BANK: **POM-POMS**

You can adjust the size of your pom-poms to suit different projects and experiment with different yarns to make dense balls or fluffier, more open pom-poms.

MATERIALS

- Yarn
- A pair of compasses
- Pencil
- Thin cardboard
- Small sharp scissors
- Tapestry needle

1 *On the cardboard, use the compasses to draw a circle the size of the pom-pom. Draw another circle inside it, about one-third of the diameter of the first. Cut out both circles to make a cardboard ring. Make a second ring in the same way.*

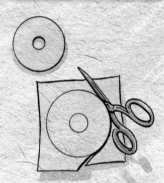

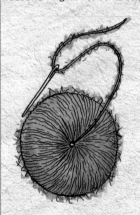

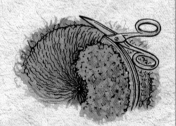

2 *Make a ball of yarn small enough to fit through the center hole. Holding the rings together, wind the yarn evenly around the ring until the center hole is filled; don't pull the yarn too tight. Thread the yarn onto a tapestry needle to finish filling the hole.*

3 *Push the scissors between the rings and cut through the yarn all the way around. Separate the rings slightly. Slip a length of yarn between them and tie it tightly.*

BOOT CUFFS

Protect your legs from the winter chill by tucking a pair of cuffs into your boots. A button adds a quick decorative flourish to these elegant accessories.

MATERIALS

- 2 x 1 oz. (25g) balls of Crea Harmony in Moonstone
- 1 x 1 oz. (25g) ball of Crea Harmony in Magma
- Pair of size 3 (3.25mm) and size 4 (3.5mm) knitting needles
- Tapestry needle
- 2 buttons, 5/8 in. (1.5cm) in diameter

SIZE

11 in. (28cm) in circumference x 6½ in. (16.5cm) long.

GAUGE

20 sts and 40 rows = 4 in. (10cm) over s st.

ABBREVIATIONS

See back flap.

TO MAKE

Using size 3 (3.25mm) needles and Moonstone, cast on 57 sts.

Rib row 1 (rs): K1, *p1, k1, rep from * to the end of the row.

Rib row 2: P1, *k1, p1, rep from * to the end of the row.

Rep these 2 rows twice more.
Change to size 4 (3.5mm) needles.
K 3 rows.

S st row: K1, *p1, k1, rep from * to the end of the row.

Rep this row until the work measures 5 in. (13cm) from the beg, ending with the ws facing.
K 3 rows.
Change to size 3 (3.25mm) needles.
Beg with Rib row 2, work 7 rows in rib, ending with Rib row 2.

Cut Moonstone and join Magma.
Change to size 4 (3.5mm) needles.
K 6 rows.
Bind off to form a decorative edge as foll:

Cast-off row: Bind off 3 sts, *with the yarn at the back, sl the next st p-wise, k into the st below the sl st but on the last row in Moonstone, then sl the first 2 sts on the right needle onto the left needle, k2tog, then lift the 2nd st on the right needle over the first st and off the needle to bind off 1 st, bind off the next 5 sts, rep from * to the end of the row, finishing the last rep bind off. 4 sts. Make another cuff in the same way.

FINISHING

Join the seam (see Knitting Basics page 92). With the seam at the center back, sew a button to the front about 1⅛ in. (3cm) from the left fold and within the top ribbing (see Café Dining, Design Bank page 61). Sew a button to the other boot cuff in the same way, but sew it about 1⅛ in. (3cm) from the right fold.

Choose contrasting colors to make a style statement.

ARM WARMERS

Keep your arms toasty but your fingers free with a pair of arm warmers. The ribbed cuff keeps them on your arms while the bramble stitch creates texture.

MATERIALS

- 5[6:6] x 1 oz. (25g) balls of Crea Antique in Slate
- Pair of size 7 (4.5mm) and size 9 (5.5mm) knitting needles
- Size H/8 (5.0mm) crochet hook
- 1 in. (2.5cm) pom-pom maker or materials to make pom-poms (see page 19)
- Tapestry needle

DESIGNER'S TIP

The long cuffs on the arm warmers can be turned back. If you are turning back the cuffs, make sure you reverse the seam for the depth of the turn-over to ensure you have a neat finish on the right side.

SIZE

7½[8¼:9] in. (19[21:23]cm) in circumference x 12¾ in. (32cm) long.

GAUGE

5 patt reps and 20 rows = 4 in. (10cm) over bramble patt.

ABBREVIATIONS

See back flap.

TO MAKE

Using size 9 (5.5mm) needles, cast on 38[42:46] sts.
Work in the bramble st patt as foll:
Row 1 (rs): P to the end of the row.
Row 2: K1, *work k1, p1 and k1 all into the next st, p3tog, rep from * to the last st, k1.
Row 3: P to the end of the row.
Row 4: K1, *p3tog, work k1, p1 and k1 all into the next st, rep from * to the last st, k1.
These 4 rows form the patt.
Cont in patt until the work measures 8 in. (20cm) from the beg, ending with Row 2 or 4.
Inc row: K3, *inc in the next st, k1, rep from * to the last st, k1. 55[61:67] sts.
Change to size 7 (4.5mm) needles.
Work the cuff as foll:
Rib row 1 (ws): K1, *p1, k1, rep from * to the end of the row.

Rib row 2: P1, *k1, p1, rep from * to the end of the row.
Rep these 2 rows until the work measures 12¾ in. (32cm) from the beg, ending with Rib row 1.
Bind off k-wise leaving a long yarn tail.

TIE: Using a crochet hook, make a ch 22 in. (56cm) long.
Fasten off. Sew in the ends.
Make 2 pom-poms 1 in. (2.5cm) in diameter (see Winter Walks Design Bank page 19).

FINISHING

Sew in the ends. Fold the arm warmer in half with right sides together; pin the seam leaving an opening for the thumb. Carefully try on and adjust the opening if necessary. Join the seam (see Knitting Basics page 92). Thread the tie through the last row in the bramble st patt to tie at the center back. Sew a pom-pom to each end of the tie.

Make another arm warmer in the same way.

great with, or without, a long-sleeved coat.

CUTE SLIPPERS

Make sure baby's feet stay cozy in a pair of slippers.
Worked in the stockinette stitch and the garter stitch, they
can be trimmed with a loafer-style tassel or a pretty bow.

MATERIALS

- Tassel slippers, 1 x 1 oz. (25g) ball of Crea Harmony in Basalt
- Bow slippers, 1 x 1 oz. (25g) ball of Crea Harmony in Moonstone
- Pair of size 4 (3.5mm) knitting needles
- Tapestry needle

SIZE
Length of foot 3⅛ in. (8cm).

GAUGE
28 sts and 44 rows = 4 in. (10cm) over g st.

ABBREVIATIONS
See back flap.

SPECIAL ABBREVIATIONS
ssk = slip, slip, knit worked as follows: sl the next 2 sts k-wise, insert the left needle into the 2 slipped sts, from left to right, and k them tog.

TO MAKE
TASSEL SLIPPERS: Using size 4 (3.5mm) needles and Basalt, cast on 11 sts for the slipper top.
K 1 row.
Beg with a k row, work 12 rows st st, ending with a p row.

The perfect handmade gift for a baby to grow into...

Cut yarn and leave the sts on the needle.
Onto an empty needle cast on 12 sts; onto same needle, with rs facing, pick up and k 11 sts along the first side of the slipper top, k the sts on the needle, pick up and k 11 sts along the second side, turn and cast on 12 sts. 57 sts.
K 9 rows, ending with ws facing.
Now shape as foll:
Row 1: K24, ssk, k5, k2tog, k to the end of the row. 55 sts.
Row 2: K23, k2tog, k5, ssk, k to the end of the row. 53 sts.
Row 3: K2, ssk, k19, ssk, k3, k2tog, k19, k2tog, k2. 49 sts.
Row 4: K to the end of the row.
Row 5: Ssk, k2, ssk, k13, (ssk, k1) twice, (k2tog, k1) twice, k12, k2tog, k2, k2tog. 41 sts.
Row 6: K to the end of the row.
Row 7: Ssk, k1, ssk, k10, (ssk, k1) twice, (k2tog, k1) twice, k9, k2tog, k1, k2tog. 33 sts.
Row 8: K to the end of the row.
Row 9: (Ssk) twice, k7, (ssk, k1) twice, (k2tog, k1) twice, k6. (k2tog) twice. 25 sts.
Row 10: K to the end of the row.
Bind off.

Make another slipper in the same way.

FINISHING

Join the back and sole seams (see Knitting Basics page 92). Weave in the ends. Cut eight 2 in. (5cm) lengths of yarn. Use four lengths of yarn to form a tassel on the top of each slipper (see Winter Walks Design Bank page 15). Trim the ends.

BOW SLIPPERS: Using Moonstone, work as given for the tassel slippers, omitting the tassels.

BOW (MAKE 2): Using size 4 (3.5mm) needles and Moonstone, cast on 11 sts.
S st row: K1, *p1, k1 rep from * to the end of the row.
Rep this row 6 more times.
Bind off in patt.

FINISHING

Join the back and sole seams. Weave in the ends. Wrap a length of yarn three times around the center of the bow strips to gather them, secure the ends on the wrong side, but do not cut the ends. Use the ends to sew a bow to the top of each slipper.

DESIGNER'S TIP

Customize your little slippers by adding a decoration along the top using French knots (see Design Bank on page 27). Sew them in a line, as shown here, work a flower shape, or try a scattering of knots.

Use scraps of yarn to finish the knitted bows and embellish the slippers with French knots.

DESIGN BANK: **FRENCH KNOTS**

French knots are isolated knotted stitches
that are used to add texture and details
or to fill in small areas.

French knots are small, circular knotted stitches that stand out from the fabric. They are used alone or in small groups to highlight a particular feature of a design, often using a contrasting weight of yarn or thread.

French knots can also be lightly scattered over an area to add color and texture, or they're worked close together to fill a shape with dense, knotted stitching. They can be a little tricky to master, so it's worth practicing them to achieve the perfect finish.

EXPERT'S TIP

When you are working individual knots, or widely spaced knots, fasten off the thread after each one. When working groups of closely spaced knots, you can carry the thread across the back of the fabric between knots instead of fastening it off after every stitch.

FRENCH KNOTS

The size and the effect produced can be varied by working with different yarns and threads.

1 *Bring the thread through to the front of the fabric. Holding the thread taut with your left hand, wrap it twice around the needle.*

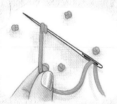

2 *Pull the thread gently to tighten the twists around the needle. Don't overtighten the twists, or you will find it difficult to slide the needle through in the next step.*

3 *Still holding the thread taut with your left hand, insert the needle into the fabric close to the point where it originally emerged. Pull the needle and thread through to the back, to leave a loose knot at the front.*

MAN'S BEANIE

To bundle up against the cold, a close-fitting hat is just the thing, and an easy-to-knit broken rib stitch ensures this man's beanie is a snug fit.

MATERIALS

- 4 x 1 oz. (25g) balls of Crea Shadow in Tuff
- Pair of size 7 (4.5mm) and size 8 (5.0mm) knitting needles
- Tapestry needle

Show your love, and skills, with this smart beanie.

SIZE
To fit 22 in. (56cm) head circumference.

GAUGE
17 sts and 24 rows = 4 in. (10cm) over the broken ribbing patt, with the patt slightly stretched.

ABBREVIATIONS
See back flap.

TO MAKE
Using size 7 (4.5mm) needles, cast on 98 sts.
Rib row 1 (rs): P2, *k1, p2, rep from * to the end of the row.
Rib row 2: K2, *p1, k2, rep from * to the end of the row.
Rep these 2 rows until work measures 1½ in. (4cm), ending with Rib row 2. Change to size 8 (5.0mm) needles. Work in the broken rib patt as foll:
Row 1 (rs): P2, *k4, p2, rep from * to the end of the row.
Row 2: K2, *p4, k2, rep from * to the end of the row.
Rows 3 and 4: Rep Rows 1 and 2.
Row 5: P3, k2, *p4, k2, rep from * to the last 3 sts, p3.
Row 6: K3, p2, *k4, p2, rep from * to the last 3 sts, k3.
Rows 7 and 8: Rep Rows 5 and 6. These 8 rows form the patt. Rep them two more times.

Shape crown
Dec row 1: K1, k2tog, *k10, k2tog, rep from * to the last 11 sts, k to the end of the row. 90 sts.
K 1 row.
Dec row 2: K1, k2tog, *k9, k2tog, rep from * to the last 10 sts, k to the end of the row. 82 sts.
K 1 row.
Dec row 3: K1, k2tog, *k8, k2tog, rep from * to the last 9 sts, k to the end of the row. 74 sts.
K 1 row.
Dec row 4: K1, k2tog, *k7, k2tog, rep from * to the last 8 sts, k to the end of the row. 66 sts.
K 1 row.
Dec row 5: K1, k2tog, *k6, k2tog, rep from * to the last 7 sts, k to the end of the row. 58 sts.
K 1 row.
Dec row 6: K1, k2tog, *k5, k2tog, rep from * to the last 6 sts, k to the end of the row. 50 sts.
K 1 row.
Dec row 7: K1, k2tog, *k4, k2tog, rep from * to the last 5 sts, k to the end of the row. 42 sts.
K 1 row.
Dec row 8: K1, k2tog, *k3, k2tog, rep from * to the last 4 sts, k to the end of the row. 34 sts.
K 1 row.

Dec row 9: K1, k2tog, *k2, k2tog, rep from * to the last 3 sts, k to the end of the row. 26 sts.
K 1 row.
Dec row 10: K1, k2tog, *k1, k2tog, rep from * to the last 2 sts, k to the end of the row. 18 sts.
K 1 row.
Dec row 11: K1, *k2tog, rep from * to last st, k1. 10 sts.
Cut the yarn leaving a long yarn tail. Thread the cut end through the sts, draw up tightly and secure the end. Do not cut the yarn but use it to join the seam.

FINISHING

Use the yarn end to join the back seam (see Knitting Basics page 92). Weave in the yarn ends.

The crown features a spiral of contrasting texture.

DESIGNER'S TIP

To get a neat finish when joining the back seams, take one stitch on each side into the seam and match the pattern rows.

ROLL-NECK SWEATER

An afternoon stroll through the fallen leaves requires a sweater. Try this classic sweater knitted in narrow stripes of alternating colors and stitches.

MATERIALS

- 8[9:11:12:14] x 1 oz. (25g) balls of Crea Provenance in Albite (A)
- 8[9:11:12:14] x 1 oz. (25g) balls of Crea Paragone in Pumice (B)
- Pair of size 3 (3.25mm) and size 4 (3.5mm) knitting needles
- 2 stitch holders
- Tapestry needle

Go to Knitting Basics pages 82–94 for advice on stitches, problem solving, and finishing your knits.

SIZES

To fit bust 32[34:36:38:40] in. (81[86:91:97:102]cm).
Actual measurement 34[35½:37½:39½:41½] in. (86[90:95:100:105]cm).
Length 18[18:19:19:19¾] in. (46[46:48:48:50]cm).
Sleeve seam 17[17:17¼:17¼:17¼] in. (43[43:44:44:44]cm).

GAUGE

19 sts and 25 rows = 4 in. (10cm) over patt.

ABBREVIATIONS

See back flap.

TO MAKE

BACK: Using size 3 (3.25mm) needles and A, cast on 82[86:90:94:98] sts.
Rib row 1 (rs): K2, *p2, k2, rep from * to the end of the row.
Rib row 2: P2, *k2, p2, rep from * to the end of the row.
Rep these 2 rows for 2 in. (5cm), ending with Rib row 2, but inc 0[0:1:1:2] sts on the last row. 82[86:91:95:100] sts.
Change to size 4 (3.5mm) needles. Now work in the alternate stripe patt as foll:

Row 1 (rs): With A, k to the end of the row.
Row 2: With A, p to the end of the row. Join B (see Knitting Basics page 89).
Row 3: With B, k to the end of the row, wrapping the yarn twice around the needle for each st.
Row 4: With B, p to the end of the row, dropping the extra loops from the previous row.
These 4 rows form the patt.
Stranding the yarns loosely up the side of the knitting, cont in the patt until the work measures 18[18:19:19:19¾] in. (46[46:48:48:50]cm) from the beg, ending with Row 4. Cut B.

EXPERT'S TIP

To work the long stitches in Rows 3 and 4, knit to the end of Row 3, winding the yarn twice around the needle for each stitch. In Row 4, insert the needle into the first stitch and purl it, letting the extra loop drop from the left needle. Purl to the end of the row, dropping the extra loop on each stitch.

Shape shoulders

Bind off 8[8:9:10:10] sts at the beg of the next 2 rows and 7[8:8:8:9] sts at the beg of the foll 4 rows.
Cut yarn leaving a long yarn tail, and leave the rem 38[38:41:43:44] sts on a holder.

FRONT:

Work as given for the back until 12 rows less than the back have been worked to the shoulders, ending with a ws row.

Shape neck

Next row: Patt 32[34:35:36:38], turn and leave the rem sts on a spare needle.
Work on the first set of sts as foll:
Dec 1 st at the neck edge on every row until 22[24:25:26:28] sts rem. Work 1 row straight, ending at the armhole edge. Cut B.

Shape shoulder

Bind off 8[8:9:10:10] sts at the beg of the next row and 7[8:8:8:9] sts at the beg of the foll row.
Work 1 row. Bind off leaving a long yarn tail.
With rs facing, place the next 18[18:21:23:24] sts on a holder, rejoin the yarn to the next st, patt to the end of the row. 32[34:35:36:38] sts.
Dec 1 st at the neck edge on every row until 22[24:25:26:28] sts rem. Work 2 rows straight, ending at the armhole edge. Cut B.

Shape shoulder

Bind off 8[8:9:10:10] sts at the beg of the next row and 7[8:8:8:9] sts at the beg of the foll row. Work 1 row. Bind off leaving a long yarn tail.

SLEEVES:

Using size 3 (3.25mm) needles and A, cast on 46[46:50:50:54] sts.
Work the 2 Rib rows of the back for 2 in. (5cm), ending with a ws row.
Change to size 4 (3.5mm) needles. Work in the patt as given for the back, but inc 1 st at each end of the 5th and every foll 8th row until there are 64[64:68:68:72] sts. Cont without shaping until the sleeve measures 17[17:17¼: 17¼: 17¼] in. (43[43:44:44:44]cm) from the beg, ending with Rib row 2.
Bind off loosely leaving a long yarn tail.

NECKBAND:

Join the right shoulder seam (see Knitting Basics page 92). With the rs facing, join A and, using size 4 (3.5mm) needles, pick up and k 12 sts along the left front neck, k the sts from the holder, pick up and k 12 sts along the right front neck, then k the back neck sts from the holder. 80[80:86:90:92] sts.
Beg with a p row, work in st st for 1¾ in. (4.5cm), ending with a p row. Bind off loosely leaving a long yarn tail.

FINISHING

Block the pieces to size using the spray method (see Knitting Basics page 94). Join the rem shoulder and neckband seam, reversing the seam for ¾ in. (2cm) on the neckband—see Designer's Tip.
Mark the depth of the armholes 6½[6½:6⅞: 6⅞:7¼] in. (16.5[16.5:17.5:17.5:18.5]cm) from the shoulder seams on the back and the front. Sew the bound-off edge of the sleeves to the armholes between the markers, then join the side and sleeve seams.

DESIGNER'S TIP

The rolled neckband is worked in stockinette stitch and rolls over to the right side. When joining the ends, reverse the seam on the top section so that it doesn't show on the right side.

The contrasting yarns and stitches knit together to create row upon row of texture.

COZY
HOME

CABLE PANEL PILLOW

Cuddle up in your favorite spot with this comfy pillow.
It is decorated with a central cable panel and the
overlap at the back is secured with a cord tie.

MATERIALS

- 6 x 1 oz. (25g) balls of Crea Impasto in Pebble
- Pair of size 6 (4.0mm) knitting needles
- Cable needle
- 13¾ in. (35cm) length of cord
- Tapestry needle
- 12 in. 30cm square pillow pad

Go to Knitting Basics pages 82–94 for advice on stitches, problem solving, and finishing your knits.

EXPERT'S TIP

If you are new to knitting cables, practice the stitches using the yarn and needles listed in the pattern and see Knitting Basics pages 90-91 for how to knit cables. Once you have worked one or two pattern repeats, you will be ready to cast on and knit the pillow.

SIZE

To fit a pillow pad 12 in. (30cm) square.

GAUGE

20 sts and 28 rows = 4 in. (10cm) over stockinette stitch.

ABBREVIATIONS

See back flap.

SPECIAL ABBREVIATIONS

C4F = cable 4 front worked as follows: sl 2 sts onto the cn and leave at the front of the work, k2, then k the sts from the cn.

C8F = cable 8 front worked as follows: sl 4 sts onto the cn and leave at the front of the work, k4, then k the sts from the cn.

TO MAKE

Using size 6 (4.0mm) needles, cast on 68 sts.
K 1 row.
Now work in st st with cable panel (see Knitting Basics page 90) as foll:
Row 1 (rs): K20, p3, k4, p3, k8, p3, k4, p3, k20.
Row 2: P20, k3, p4, k3, p8, k3, p4, k3, p20.
Row 3: K20, p3, C4F, p3, C8F, p3, C4F, p3, k20.
Row 4: Rep Row 2.
Rows 5 and 6: Rep Rows 1 and 2.
Row 7: K20, p3, C4F, p3, k8, p3, C4F, p3, k20.
Row 8: Rep Row 2.
These 8 rows form the patt.

This plump pillow cover is knitted in a neutral shade that will suit any decor.

Cont in the patt until the work measures 27½ in. (70cm), ending with Row 4.

M st row 1: *K1, p1, rep from * to the end of the row.

M st row 2: *P1, k1, rep from * to the end of the row.

Rep these 2 rows once more, then work the s st row 1 again. Bind off k-wise leaving a long yarn tail.

FINISHING

Block your knitting (see Knitting Basics page 94). Place the knitting with the right side facing on a flat surface and fold the top, bind-off edge down, then fold the bottom up, overlapping knitting for 2⅜ in. (6cm). Pin the side edges, then join the side seams, working through all three layers at the overlap (see Knitting Basics page 92).

Turn the cover through to the right side and insert the pillow pad. Thread a cord through the layers at the center of the overlap and tie a bow to secure it.

EXPERT'S TIP

Take your time when you pin and sew the side edges together to make sure the cables are aligned on the back of the finished pillow cover.

A neat cord bow secures the pad inside the cover and adds a design flourish.

COZY SHRUG

Slip on this gorgeous cover-up to keep shoulders warm and look great too. Knitted in garter stitch in a chunky yarn, it is created from a simple T-shape by joining two seams.

The turned-back collar hugs your neck to keep it toasty.

SIZES

To fit bust 32[34:36:38:40] in. (81[86:91:97:102]cm).
Length 11¾[12½:13¼:14:15] in. (30[32:34:36:38]cm).

GAUGE

15 sts and 26 rows = 4 in. (10cm) over g st.

ABBREVIATIONS

See back flap.

TO MAKE (MADE IN ONE PIECE)

Using size 10½ (6.5mm) needles, cast on 45[48:51:54:57] sts.
Work in g st (every row k) until the work measures 11[11¾:12½:13¾:15] in. (28[30:32:35:38]cm) from the cast-on edge.

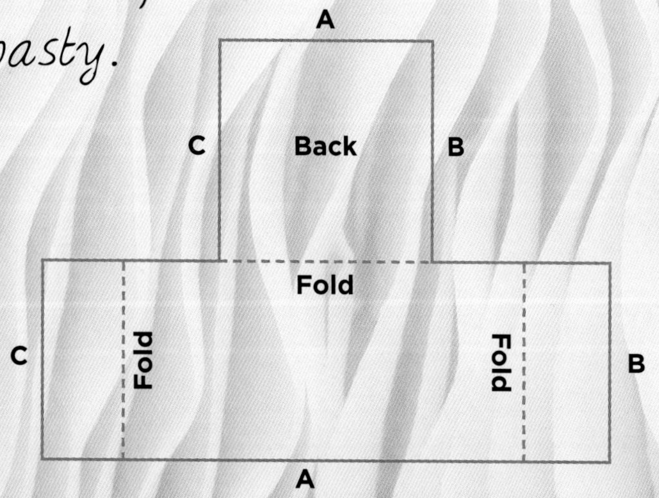

Next row: Cast on 45[48:51:54:57] sts for the back. 90[96:102:108:114] sts.
Cont straight in g st until the work measures 12½ [14:15¾:17¼:19] in. (32[36:40:44:48]cm) from the cast-on sts for the back, ending at the back edge.

Next row: Bind off 45[48:51:54:57] sts to complete the back, k to the end of the row. 45[48:51:54:57] sts.
Cont straight in g st until the work measures 11[11¾:12½:13¾:15] in. (28[30:32:35:38]cm) from the bound-off row. Bind off leaving a long yarn tail.

FINISHING

Place the knitting on a flat surface with the back section at the top. Fold the back section down so that the row ends are level (see A to A in diagram below). Pin the cast-on edge to the cast-on edge of the back (B to B). Now pin the bound-off edge to the bound-off edge of the back (C to C). Join the seams (see Knitting Basics page 92). The lower edge will be open and you will have an opening at each side on the top edge for the armholes. Fold back the edge to form the collar.

A

C **Back** B

Fold

C **Fold** **Fold** B

A

HOODED BLANKET

This hooded blanket will wrap around baby to keep them snug and warm. It is knitted in a soft, chunky yarn that will be gentle on young skin.

MATERIALS

- 19 x 1 oz. (25g) balls of Crea Antique in Ivory
- Size 10½ (6.5mm) circular needle, 31½ in. (80cm) long
- Pair of size 10½ (6.5mm) needles
- Tapestry needle

Go to Knitting Basics pages 82–94 for advice on stitches, problem solving, and finishing your knits.

The rows of knit and purl stitches create a plush surface.

SIZE

39½ in. (100cm) wide x 27½ in. (70cm) long, excluding hood.

GAUGE

13 sts and 26 rows = 4 in. (10cm) over patt.

ABBREVIATIONS

See back flap.

SPECIAL ABBREVIATIONS

ssk = slip, slip, knit worked as follows: sl the next 2 sts k-wise, insert the left needle into the 2 slipped sts, from left to right, and k them tog.

TO MAKE

BLANKET: Using a size 10½ (6.5mm) circular needle, cast on 130 sts. Working forward and backward in rows, k 5 rows.
Now work in patt as foll:
Row 1 (rs): K to the end of the row.
Rows 2 and 3: P to the end of the row.
Row 4: K to the end of the row.
These 4 rows form the patt.
Cont in the patt until the work measures 26⅜ in. (67cm) from the beg, ending with Row 2.
P 5 rows.

Next row: Bind off 44 sts k-wise, p until there are 42 sts on the needle, bind off the rem 44 sts k-wise and fasten off.

HOOD: With the rs facing, rejoin the yarn to the 42 sts on the circular needle.
Cont in g st (every row k) on pair of size 10½ (6.5mm) needles, shaping as foll:
Row 1: K17, puk, k8, puk, k to the end of the row. 44 sts.
Row 2: K to the end of the row.
Row 3: K17, puk, k10, puk, k to the end of the row. 46 sts.
Row 4: K to the end of the row.
Row 5: K17, puk, k12, puk, k to the end of the row. 48 sts.
Row 6: K to the end of the row.
Row 7: K17, puk, k14, puk, k to the end of the row. 50 sts.
Row 8: K to the end of the row.
Row 9: K17, puk, k16, puk, k to the end of the row. 52 sts.
Cont without shaping until the hood measures 7½ in. (19cm), ending with the ws facing.
Next row (rs): K17, ssk, k14, k2tog, k to the end of the row. 50 sts.
Next row: K to the end of the row.

Next row: K17, ssk, k12, k2tog, k to the end of the row. 48 sts.

Next row: K to the end of the row.

Next row: K17, ssk, k10, k2tog, k to the end of the row. 46 sts.

Next row: K to the end of the row.

Next row: K17, ssk, k8, k2tog, k to the end of the row. 44 sts.

Next row: K to the end of the row.

Next row: K17, ssk, k6, k2tog, k to the end of the row. 42 sts.

Next row: K to the end of the row.

Next row: K17, ssk, k4, k2tog, k to the end of the row. 40 sts. Bind off leaving a long yarn tail.

FINISHING

Fold the hood in half and join the bind-off edge to form a seam (see Knitting Basics page 92). Weave in the yarn ends.

DESIGNER'S TIP

The blanket is worked in rows on a circular needle. If you prefer to use a pair of knitting needles you will need a long pair to accommodate the number of stitches comfortably.

SKINNY SCARF

This delicate lace scarf is just the thing as a versatile neck warmer. It is worked in a simple zigzag lace pattern and then finished with a luxurious yarn fringe.

MATERIALS

- 2 x 2 oz. (50g) balls of Crea Harmony in Cyclamen
- Pair of size 4 (3.5mm) knitting needles
- Tapestry needle

Go to Knitting Basics pages 82–94 for advice on stitches, problem solving, and finishing your knits.

DESIGNER'S TIP

The scarf fabric will roll at the side edges to give it the skinny look. If you prefer a flat fabric, simply block your scarf to size using the wet method and let it dry completely (see Knitting Basics page 94).

SIZE

7½ in. (19cm) wide x 45½ in. (116cm) long, excluding tassels.

GAUGE

25 sts and 32 rows = 4 in. (10cm) over zigzag lace patt.

ABBREVIATIONS

See back flap.

TO MAKE

Using size 4 (3.5mm) needles, cast on 47 sts.
Work in the zigzag lace patt as folls:
Row 1 (rs): K2, *skpo, k2, yfd, k2, rep from * to the last 3 sts, k3.
Row 2: K2, p to the last 2 sts, k2.
Rows 3 to 6: Rep Rows 1 and 2 two times.

Row 7: K5, *yfd, k2, k2tog, k2, rep from * to the last 6 sts, yfd, k2, k2tog, k2.
Row 8: K2, p to the last 2 sts, k2.
Rows 9 to 12: Rep Rows 7 and 8 two times.
These 12 rows form the patt.
Cont in patt until the work measures 45½ in. (116cm) from the beg, ending with Row 12 of the patt.
Bind off k-wise.

FINISHING

Weave in the ends. Using three 9½-in. (24cm-) lengths of yarn together, knot a fringe into each eyelet closest to the cast-on and bind-off edges (see Cozy Home, Design Bank page 47). Trim the ends.

A lace scarf gives you a pretty extra layer without being bulky.

DESIGN BANK: **FRINGE**

Fringes add extra embellishment to items
as diverse as scarves, throws, and even pillow covers.
Make them as long as you like.

The key to a successful fringe is even spacing. Always measure the length of the edge to be fringed and space the individual knots evenly, marking their positions with pins before you start.

Calculate the length of fringe you want and wind the yarn around a piece of cardboard at least 2 in. (5cm) deeper. Slip scissors between the yarn and the cardboard and snip through the base of the loops. Use a crochet hook or bobby pin to knot your fringe onto the fabric.

EXPERT'S TIP

Cords and ribbons make an attractive fringe and can be used as alternatives to knitting yarns. Check that the material you use is washable and remove it before laundering if necessary.

WORKING FRINGE

Depending how thick your fringe material and how bold you want the finished result, use two to six strands for each section.

1 *Insert a crochet hook through the edge of the fabric from the back to the front. Fold a group of strands in half, place them over the hook and pull through to the back leaving a loop. Pass the yarn ends through the loop and pull gently to tighten the knot.*

2 *Lay the finished fringe flat and trim off the ends evenly to the required length. If you are trimming a wide fringe, use low-tack masking tape to secure it to a flat surface, then trim the fringe. Carefully remove the masking tape.*

• For a plump fringe, use shorter lengths and place the fringes close together. For a different look, try fluffing up the yarn with a small stiff brush to form tufts.

LITTLE TEDDY

This adorable teddy is the perfect size for little hands. It is knitted in the stockinette stitch and finished with embroidered features and a smart bow tie.

MATERIALS

- 2 x 1 oz. (25g) balls of Crea Impasto in Zircon
- Pair of size 4 (3.5mm) knitting needles
- Tapestry needle
- Washable toy filling
- Scrap of dark gray yarn for features

EXPERT'S TIP

Be sure to check your gauge for this toy. If the stitches are too loose, the filling may escape through any gaps in the stitches.

SIZE

7 in. (18cm) high.

GAUGE

22 sts and 30 rows = 4 in. (10cm) over st st.

ABBREVIATIONS

See back flap.

TO MAKE

BACK: Using size 4 (3.5mm) needles, cast on 10 sts for the first leg.
Beg with a k row, work 10 rows st st, ending with a p row.
Cut yarn and leave the sts on the needle.
Onto the needle holding the first leg, cast on 10 sts for the second leg.
Beg with a k row, work 10 rows st st, ending with a p row.
Next row: K to the end of the row, cast on 3 sts, then k across the sts of the first leg. 23 sts.
Beg with a p row, work 15 rows st st.
Shape armholes
Next row: K1, skpo, k to the last 3 sts, k2tog, k1.
Next row: P to the end of the row.
Rep these 2 rows four more times. 13 sts.
Bind off leaving a long yarn tail.

FRONT

Work as given for the back.

ARMS (make 2): Using size 4 (3.5mm) needles, cast on 14 sts.
Beg with a k row, work 12 rows st st.
Shape top
Next row: K1, skpo, k to the last 3 sts, k2tog, k1.
Next row: P to the end of the row.
Rep these 2 rows three more times. 6 sts.
Next row: K1, skpo, k2tog, k1. 4 sts.
Next row: P to the end of the row.
Bind off leaving a long yarn tail.

HEAD

Back: Using size 4 (3.5mm) needles, cast on 11 sts.
K 1 row and p 1 row.
Inc row: K1, k into the front, back, then front again of the next st, *k3, k into the front, back, then front again of the next st, rep from * to the last st, k1. 17 sts.
Beg with a p row, work 15 rows st st.
Shape top
Dec 1 st at each end of the next and the foll alt row. 13 sts.
Work 1 row.
Bind off, working the first and last 2 sts tog and leaving a long yarn tail.
Front: Work as given for the back.

BOW

Using size 4 (3.5mm) needles, cast on 6 sts.
Work in g st (every row k) for 1½ in. (4cm). Bind off leaving a long yarn tail.
Using size 4 (3.5mm) needles, cast on 30 sts for tie, then bind off leaving a long yarn tail.

FINISHING

Join the top shaping on each arm to the armhole shaping on the back and front of the body (see Knitting Basics page 92). With the right sides together, sew around the outer edge of the arms, body, and legs, leaving the top of the body open. Turn right side out. Insert the toy filling into the arms, legs, and body.

With right sides facing, sew the head pieces together, leaving the lower edge open, turn right side out. Insert the toy filling, then sew the head to the body. Sew diagonally across the corners of the head to form the ears. Use the gray yarn to embroider the eyes, nose, mouth, and buttons (see Designer's Tip below).

Knot the tie round the center of the bow, place around the neck of the teddy and join the ends securely.

DESIGNER'S TIP

Embroider the smiley face working a French knot (see Winter Walks, Design Bank page 27) or two straight stitches for each eye, a group of straight stitches for the nose, and three long stitches for the mouth. For the buttons, work three cross stitches on the body (see Design Bank page 51). Secure all the yarn ends on the inside of the teddy.

The teddy's smiling face will ensure it's a favorite toy.

This is a simple but effective way to add surface decoration to knitted fabrics. You can work single crosses, rows, blocks, or a motif.

Plain knits are ideal for the cross stitch—the V-shapes of stockinette stitch can be used in the same way as the blocks or threads in an evenweave fabric. However, crosses can be worked freehand on textured, knitted fabrics—just make sure you work all the stitches the same size. Always secure the ends of the thread on the wrong side of the fabric.

You can use cross stitch charts, though large motifs may be a little distorted as the grid formed by the knitted stitches is not perfectly square—you can correct the distortion by adding extra stitches to the height of the chart.

WORKING CROSS STITCH

Here's how to work cross stitch on a stockinette stitch fabric.

1 *Mark the bottom right-hand stitch of the design with a safety pin. Insert the needle 1 in. (2.5cm) below the pin and bring it out at the bottom left of the marked stitch, leaving a 2 in. (5cm) tail. Make the first diagonal of the cross over the knitted stitch. Bring the needle out at the top left of the stitch.*

2 *Take out the safety pin. Work a second diagonal to complete the first cross stitch. Bring the needle out at the bottom left of the next knitted stitch to the left.*

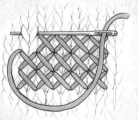

3 *Continue in this way along the row. Work more rows directly above, so that the base of the stitches on the row above share the same holes as the top of the stitches on the row below.*

BOYFRIEND CARDIGAN

Pull on this chic, loose-fitting cardigan when you need to keep out the chill. It is knitted in an easy-to-remember textured stitch and has set-in sleeves.

MATERIALS

- 38[41:44] x 1 oz. (25g) balls of Crea Shadow in Gabbro
- Pair each of size 7 (4.5mm) and size 8 (5.0mm) knitting needles
- 8 stitch markers
- Tapestry needle
- 6 buttons, ¾ in. (2cm) in diameter

Go to Knitting Basics pages 82–94 for advice on stitches, problem solving, and finishing your knits.

This loose-fitting cardigan is the epitome of casual chic.

SIZES

To suit bust 32–34[36–38:40–42] in. (81–86[91–97:102–107]cm).
Actual measurement 41¾[47:51½] in. (106[119:131]cm).
Length 28[29½:30] in. (71[75:76]cm).
Sleeve seam 18½[19:19] in. (47[48:48]cm).

GAUGE

39 sts = 8 in. (20cm) and 30 rows = 4 in. (10cm) over patt.

ABBREVIATIONS

See back flap.

TO MAKE

BACK: Using size 7 (4.5mm) needles, cast on 104[116:128] sts.
Rib row: *K1, p1, rep from * to the end of the row.
Rep this row 5 more times.
Change to size 8 (5.0mm) needles.
Now work in the patt as foll:
Row 1 (rs): P2, *with the yarn at the back, sl 1 k-wise, p2, rep from * to the end of the row.
Row 2: K2, *with the yarn at the front, sl 1 p-wise, k2, rep from * to the end of the row.
Row 3: K to the end of the row.
Row 4: P to the end of the row.
These 4 rows form the patt.**
Cont in the patt until the work measures 19½[20½:20½] in. (50[52:52]cm) from the beg, ending with Row 4.
Place a marker at each end of the last row to denote the armholes.

Shape armholes

Keeping the patt correct, dec 1 st at each end of the next and every foll row until 96[106:116] sts rem.
Cont without shaping until the armholes measure 8¼[9:9½] in. (21[23:24]cm), ending with a ws row.

Shape shoulders

Bind off 16[18:19] sts at the beg of the next 2 rows and 16[19:20] sts at the beg of the foll 2 rows.
Bind off the rem 32[32:38] sts leaving a long yarn tail.

LEFT FRONT: Using size 7 (4.5mm) needles, cast on 50[56:62] sts.
Work as given for the back from ** to **.
Cont in the patt until the work measures 4 rows less than back to the armholes, ending with Row 4.

Shape front edge

Keeping the patt correct, dec 1 st at the end (for the right front at the beg) on the next and the foll alt row. 48[54:60] sts.

Patt 1 row.

Place a marker at the end (for right front at the beg) of the last row to denote the armhole.

Shape armhole

Keeping the patt correct, cont to dec at the front edge on every alt row, at the same time dec 1 st at the armhole edge on the next and every foll alt row until 40[44:48] sts rem.

Keeping the armhole edge straight, dec at the front edge on every 4th row until 32[37:39] sts rem.

Cont without shaping until the armhole measures 8¼[9:9½] in. (21[23:24]cm), ending at the armhole edge.

Shape shoulder

Bind off 16[18:19] sts at the beg of the next row.

Work 1 row. Bind off leaving a long yarn tail.

RIGHT FRONT: Work as given for the left front noting the bracketed exceptions.

SLEEVES: Using size 7 (4.5mm) needles, cast on 44[47:47] sts.

Rep the Rib row of the back 12 times. Change to size 8 (5.0mm) needles. Work in the patt as given for the back, but inc 1 st at each end of the next and every foll 6th row until there are 74[81:85] sts.

Cont without shaping until the sleeve measures 18½[19:19] in. (47[48:48]cm) from the beg, ending with a ws row.

Place a marker at each end of the last row to denote the top of the sleeve.

Shape top

Keeping the patt correct, dec 1 st at each end of the next 5[6:6] rows. 64[69:73] sts.

Work 3 rows without shaping. Now bind off 4 sts at the beg of the next 14[14:15] rows. 8[11:11] sts.

Work 2 rows without shaping. Bind off leaving a long yarn tail.

The simple pattern is created by slipping stitches.

BAND: Join the shoulder seams (see Knitting Basics page 92). Using size 7 (4.5mm) needles, cast on 7 sts.

Rib row 1 (rs): K2, p1, k1, p1, k2.

Rib row 2: (K1, p1) 3 times, k1.

Rep these 2 rows once more.

Buttonhole row 1 (rs): Rib 2, bind off 2, rib to the end of the row.

Buttonhole row 2: Rib to the end of the row, casting on 2 sts over those bound off on the previous row.

Work 22 rows.

Rep last 24 rows five more times. Now cont in rib until the band, when slightly stretched, fits up one front, around the neck and down the other front, ending with a ws row. Bind off leaving a long yarn tail.

FINISHING

Block pieces to size using the spray method (see Knitting Basics page 94). Matching the markers, sew the sleeves to the armholes, then join the side and sleeve seams.

Sew on the band, then sew on the buttons to correspond with the buttonholes.

DESIGNER'S TIP

This loose-fitting boyfriend-style cardigan can be fastened left over right, or right over left. Just sew the buttonhole section of the band to the front you prefer.

DESIGN BANK: **BUTTONHOLES**

Buttonholes need to work with the style of your garment and be the correct size for your buttons. Follow the steps to create the perfect buttonholes on knitted fabrics.

HORIZONTAL BUTTONHOLES

Start by knitting the stitches, then bind off the number of stitches indicated to make the buttonhole.

  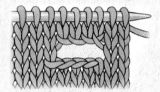

1 *On the first row, knit to the position of the buttonhole. Slip the next stitch purlwise, then knit the next stitch. Insert the left needle into the slipped stitch and lift it over the knitted stitch to bind off 1 stitch.*

2 *Knit the next stitch, then lift the previous stitch on the right needle over this stitch to bind off a second stitch. Bind off the number of stitches required and complete the row.*

3 *On the second row, work to the bound-off stitches, then cast on the same number of stitches that were bound off on the previous row; complete the row.*

ROUND BUTTONHOLES

If you want to use a very small button—on a baby's garment, for example—you can make a simple one-stitch buttonhole.

 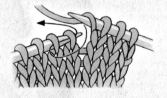 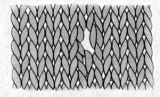

1 *On a knit row, bring the yarn to the front of the work—yarn forward. The yarn forward will lay over the right needle when you work the next stitch, so making a stitch.*

2 *Insert the right needle in the second stitch on the left needle, then insert it in the first stitch and knit the 2 stitches together.*

3 *On the following row, knit the yarn forward as a stitch. You now have a small buttonhole.*

CAFÉ
DINING

STRIPED NECK WARMER

Wear this soft and cozy neck warmer to provide an extra layer of insulation. The contrasting smooth and bouclé yarns create colored and textured stripes.

MATERIALS

- 2 x 1 oz. (25g) balls of Crea Harmony in Moonstone
- 3 x 1 oz. (25g) balls of Crea Grisaille in Moss
- Pair of size 4 (3.5mm) knitting needles
- Tapestry needle
- 3 buttons

DESIGNER'S TIP

Personalize your neck warmer by finishing it with mismatched buttons. Look for suitable examples in your button box.

SIZE

10⅝ in. (27cm) at widest point x approximately 31½ in. (80cm).

GAUGE

17 sts = 4 in. (10cm) and 3 patt reps (24 rows) = 3½ in. (9cm).

ABBREVIATIONS

See back flap.

TO MAKE

Using size 4 (3.5mm) needles and Harmony, cast on 29 sts. K 6 rows. Work the buttonholes (see Cozy Home Design Bank page 55).

Buttonhole row 1: K6, bind off 3 sts, (k until there are 4 sts on the needle after the bind off, bind off 3 sts) two times, k to the end of the row.

Buttonhole row 2: K6, cast on 3 sts, (k4, cast on 3 sts) two times, k6. 29 sts. K 3 rows.

Now work in alternating stripes of Grisaille and Harmony with g st borders (see Knitting Basics page 85). **Note:** When using Grisaille, work the rs rows wrapping the yarn twice around needle for each st and on ws rows drop the extra loops from the previous row.

Row 1 (rs): With Grisaille, k to the end of the row.

Row 2: With Grisaille, k4, p23, k2.

Rows 3 and 4: Rep Rows 1 and 2. Stranding the yarn not in use loosely up the side of the work, shape as foll:

Row 5: With Harmony, k to the end of the row.

Row 6: With Harmony, k4, p23, inc in the next st, k to the end of the row. 30 sts.

Rows 7 and 8: Rep Rows 5 and 6. 31 sts.

Row 9: With Grisaille, k to the end of the row.

Row 10: With Grisaille, k4, p23, inc in the next st, k to the end of the row. 32 sts.

Rows 11 and 12: Rep Rows 9 and 10. 33 sts.

Rows 13 to 16: Rep Rows 5 and 6 twice. 35 sts.

Row 17: With Grisaille, k to the end of the row.

Row 18: With Grisaille, k4, p23, k to the end of the row.

Row 19: With Grisaille, k to the end of the row.

Row 20: With Grisaille, k4, p23, inc in the next st, k to the end of the row. 36 sts.

Row 21: With Harmony, k to the end of the row.
Row 22: With Harmony, k4, p23, k to the end of the row.
Row 23: With Harmony, k to the end of the row.
Row 24: With Harmony, k4, p23, inc in the next st, k to the end of the row. 37 sts.
Rows 25 to 32: Rep Rows 17 to 24. 39 sts.
Row 33: With Grisaille, k to the end of the row.
Row 34: With Grisaille, k4, p23, k to the end of the row.
Rows 35 and 36: Rep Rows 33 and 34.
Row 37: With Harmony, k to the end of the row.
Row 38: With Harmony, k4, p23, k to the end of the row.
Row 39: With Harmony, k to the end of the row.
Row 40: With Harmony, k4, p23, inc in the next st, k to the end of the row. 40 sts.
Rows 41 to 72: Rep Rows 33 to 40 four times more. 44 sts.
Row 73: With Grisaille, k to the end of the row.
Row 74: With Grisaille, k4, p23, k to the end of the row.
Row 75: With Grisaille, k to last 27 sts, turn.
Row 76: With Grisaille, k to the end of the row.
Row 77: With Grisaille, k across all sts.
Row 78: With Grisaille, k4, p23, k to the end of the row.
Row 79: With Harmony, k to the end of the row.
Row 80: With Harmony, k4, p23, k to the end of the row.

Row 81: With Harmony, k to the last 27 sts, turn.
Row 82: With Harmony, k to the end of the row.
Row 83: With Harmony, k across all sts.
Row 84: With Harmony, K4, p23, k to the end of the row.
Rows 85 to 92: Rep Rows 33 to 40. 45 sts.
Rows 93 to 128: Rep Rows 73 to 84 three times.
Rows 129 to 134: Rep Rows 73 to 78.
Row 135: With Harmony, k all sts.
Row 136: With Harmony, k4, p23, k2tog, k to the end of the row. 44 sts.
Row 137: With Harmony, k all sts.
Row 138: With Harmony, k4, p23, k to the end of the row.
Row 139: With Grisaille, k to the end of the row.
Row 140: With Grisaille, k4, p23, k to the end of the row.
Rows 141 and 142: Rep Rows 139 and 140.
Rows 143 to 148: Rep Rows 79 to 84.
Rows 149 to 154: Rep Rows 73 to 78.
Rows 155 to 158: Rep Rows 135 to 138. 43 sts.
Rows 159 to 162: Rep Rows 33 to 36.
Rows 163 to 194: Rep Rows 135 to 142 four times. 39 sts.
Rows 195 to 198: Rep Rows 135 to 138. 38 sts.
Row 199: With Grisaille, k to the end of the row.
Row 200: With Grisaille, k4, p23, k2tog, k to the end of the row. 37 sts.

Row 201: With Grisaille, k to the end of the row.
Row 202: With Grisaille, k4, p23, k to the end of the row.
Row 203: With Harmony, k to the end of the row.
Row 204: With Harmony, k4, p23, k2tog, k to the end of the row. 36 sts.
Row 205: With Harmony, k to the end of the row.
Row 206: With Harmony, k4, p23, k to the end of the row.
Row 207 to 210: Rep Rows 199 to 202. 35 sts.
Row 211: With Harmony, k to the end of the row.
Row 212: With Harmony, k4, p23, k2tog, k to the end of the row. 34 sts.
Rows 213 and 214: Rep Rows 211 and 212. 33 sts.
Row 215: With Grisaille, k to the end of the row.
Row 216: With Grisaille, k4, p23, k2tog, k to the end of the row. 32 sts.
Rows 217 and 218: Rep Rows 215 and 216. 31 sts.
Rows 219 to 222: Rep Rows 211 to 214. 29 sts.
Row 223: With Grisaille, k to the end of the row.
Row 224: With Grisaille, k4, p23, k to the end of the row.
Rows 225 and 226: Rep Rows 223 and 224.
Cut Grisaille.
Rows 227 to 236: With Harmony, k to the end of the row. Bind off leaving a long yarn tail.

FINISHING
Weave in the ends. Sew on buttons (see Design Bank on page 61).

DESIGN BANK: **ADDING BUTTONS**

Buttons can be used as a simple fastening
or as a decorative feature. To keep it secure,
attach a four-hole button with a cross.

Buttons are most commonly used as fastenings, but they can also be used to add decorative finishes to garments, accessories, and soft furnishings.

Choose from the wide variety of colors and styles available to add a personal touch to your projects or ready-made items. Remember to make sure your buttons are washable. If not they will have to be removed before washing.

EXPERT'S TIP

To sew on a button with two holes, secure the yarn on the wrong side, bring the needle to the front through one hole, and take it through the other hole to the back. Do this a couple of times, then secure the yarn on the wrong side.

MAKING A CROSS OVER FOUR HOLES

Any size button with four holes can be secured
with a simple cross.

1 *Using a length of yarn or thread, secure on the wrong side with a small stitch in the position of the button. Bring the needle up through one hole.*

2 *Take the needle down through the hole diagonally opposite to form the first half of the cross.*

3 *Bring the needle up through the hole below, then down through the hole diagonally opposite to complete the cross. Work another cross, then work a few stitches on the wrong side to fasten off.*

MUG COZIES

Knit a set of chic mug cozies for you, your family, and your friends. There are four simple designs, and they are a great way for beginners to try new stitches.

MATERIALS

- 1 x 1 oz. (25g) ball of Crea Harmony in Moonstone and Magma for the set of four mug cozies
- Pair of size 3 (3.25mm), size 5 (3.75mm), and size 8 (5.0mm) knitting needles
- Cable needle
- Tapestry needle

Go to Knitting Basics pages 82–94 for advice on stitches, problem solving, and finishing your knits.

EXPERT TIP

When knitting with two strands of yarn, make sure you pick up both when you work each stitch.

SIZES

Striped, 7 in. (18cm) in circumference x 1½ in. (4cm) long.
Two-color ribbed, 7 in. (18cm) in circumference x 1¾ in. (4.5cm) long.
Cream, 7 in. (18cm) in circumference x 1½ in. (4cm) long.
Cable, 20cm in circumference x 1¾ in. (4.5cm) long.

GAUGE

22 sts and 45 rows = 4 in. (10cm) over g st on size 5 (3.75mm) needles.
18 sts and 24 rows = 4 in. (10cm) over rib on size 8 (5.0mm) needles.
30 sts and 30 rows = 4 in. (10cm) over cable patt on size 5 (3.75mm) needles.
Note: For the two-color ribbed version, 2 strands of yarn are held together throughout.

ABBREVIATIONS

See back flap.

SPECIAL ABBREVIATION

C6F = cable 6 front worked as follows: sl 3 sts onto the cn and leave at the front of the work, k3, then k the sts from the cn.

TO MAKE

STRIPED MUG COZY

Using size 3 (3.25mm) needles and Magma, cast on 42 sts.
K 3 rows.
Join Moonstone (see Knitting Basics page 89).
Stranding the color not in use loosely up the side of the knitting, work in g st (every row k) in stripes as foll:
With Moonstone, k 4 rows.
Change to size 5 (3.75mm) needles.
K 4 rows Magma and 4 rows Moonstone.
Cut Moonstone.
K 3 rows Magma. Bind off leaving a long yarn tail.
Join seam (see Knitting Basics page 92).

These little cozies will help to protect fingers from the heat.

TWO-COLOR RIBBED MUG COZY

Using size 8 (5.0mm) needles and one strand each of Moonstone and Magma held tog, cast on 34 sts.

Row 1 (rs): P2, *k2, p2, rep from * to the end of the row.

Row 2: K2, *p2, k2, rep from * to the end of the row.

Rep these 2 rows four mroe times, then work Row 1 again.

Bind off k-wise leaving a long yarn tail.

Join the seam.

CREAM MUG COZY

Using size 3 (3.25mm) needles and Moonstone, cast on 42 sts.

K 7 rows.

Change to size 5 (3.75mm) needles.

K 11 rows. Bind off leaving a long yarn tail.

Join the seam.

Bobble: Using size 3 (3.25mm) needles and Moonstone, cast on 6 sts.

K 10 rows. Cut the yarn leaving a 8 in. (20cm) tail. Thread the end onto a tapestry needle and thread through the sts on the knitting needle; remove the needle. Work a row of small running sts along the first side of the strip, across the cast-on edge, then along the second side of the strip; pull up to form a bobble and secure the end. Sew the bobble to the top of the seam (see also Design Bank on page 65).

CABLE MUG COZY

Using size 3 (3.25mm) needles and Magma, cast on 62 sts.

Row 1 (rs): P3, k6, *p4, k6, rep from * to the last 3 sts, p3.

Row 2: K3, p6, *k4, p6, rep from * to the last 3 sts, k3.

Rows 3 and 4: Rep Rows 1 and 2. Change to size 5 (3.75mm) needles.

Row 5: P3, C6F, *p4, C6F, rep from * to the last 3 sts, p3 (see Knitting Basics page 90).

Row 6: Rep Row 2.

Rows 7 and 8: Rep Rows 1 and 2. These 8 rows form the patt.

Cont with size 5 (3.75mm) needles, rep the 8 patt rows once more.

Bind off leaving a long yarn tail.

Join the seam.

DESIGNER'S TIP

Make sure your mug cozy fits tightly around your cup to prevent the cup from slipping and spilling the liquid.

Add designer panache to your projects with three-dimensional bobbles. This simple garter stitch, drawstring style, is just so easy.

Decorative bobbles add unique character to a knitted project, taking it to a new design level. Garments and items for the home, such as pillows and throws, can all benefit from a touch of the unexpected.

Here we feature a knitted bobble worked separately that can be added to knitted fabrics as work progresses, or attached to knitted fabrics or ready-made items. Work in a color to match the main fabric, use tonal colors to complement the main color, or contrasting colors for added interest.

GARTER STITCH DRAWSTRING BOBBLES

Form small strips of garter stitch into lovely textured bobbles.

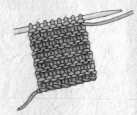

1 *Cast on 8 stitches and work 12 rows in garter stitch—every row knit.*

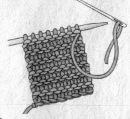

2 *Cut the yarn 4¾ in. (12cm) from the last stitch and thread the yarn tail into a large-eyed tapestry needle.*

3 *Thread the needle through the stitches on the knitting needle. Pull the yarn through and carefully remove the knitting needle.*

4 *Work small running stitches down the first side of the bobble strip, across the cast-on edge, then along the second side.*

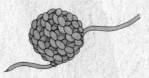

5 *Pull up the yarn to gather the knitting and form the bobble. Work a few stitches at the back of the bobble to secure the yarn. Do not cut the yarn tail but use it to sew the bobble in place.*

MESSENGER BAG

This chic, tweed bag sits comfortably across the body. It is knitted in the reverse stockinette stitch and has a long strap worked in a chunky cable stitch.

MATERIALS

- 8 x 1 oz. (25g) balls of Crea Provenance in Granite
- Pair of size 8 (5.0mm) knitting needles
- Cable needle
- Tapestry needle

SIZE

9 x 8 in. (23 x 20cm), excluding handle.

GAUGE

16 sts and 23 rows = 4 in. (10cm) over rev st st.

Note: Use 2 strands of yarn held together throughout. Wind 2 balls together before using to obtain an even gauge.

ABBREVIATIONS

See back flap.

SPECIAL ABBREVIATION

C6F = cable 6 front worked as follows: sl 3 sts onto the cn and leave at the front of the work, k3, then k the sts from the cn (see also Knitting Basics page 90).

TO MAKE

FRONT: Using size 8 (5.0mm) needles and 2 strands of yarn held together, cast on 33 sts.

Beg with a p row, work in rev st st for 8 in. (20cm), ending with a k row. K 7 rows.

Next row: Bind off 22 sts, (k2, puk) twice, k3, bind off the last 3 sts.

With rs facing, rejoin the 2 strands of yarn to the rem 10 sts and work the strap as foll:

Row 1 (rs): K to the end of the row.
Row 2: K2, p6, k2.
Rows 3 to 6: Rep Rows 1 and 2 twice.
Row 7: K2, C6F, k2.
Row 8: K2, p6, k2.
These 8 rows form the patt.
Rep them 15 more times, then work Rows 1 and 2 again. Bind off leaving a long yarn tail.

BACK: Work as given for the front.

FINISHING

Join the side and lower seams, then join the bound-off edge of the straps together (see Knitting Basics page 92).
Press the seams.

EXPERT TIP

When knitting cables, always slip stitches onto the cable needle purlwise to avoid twisting them.

This bag is just the right size to hold what you need when you're going to the café.

DESIGN BANK: **RUNNING STITCH**

The running stitch is one of the basic straight stitches used in embroidery. It can be worked with different materials—from fine cotton to textured ribbons.

Running stitch is a simple but effective stitch that can be used alone for linear designs, to outline shapes, and to add details to designs.

Plan your design before you start, then work it on the fabric freehand. Alternatively, use a water-soluble or air-erasable marker pen to transfer the design. If you are using a marker pen, test it on a small piece of fabric first.

Use a material that complements your knitted fabric, but one that isn't too chunky or wide, as this will distort the knitting. Work into or between the stitches and rows, and make sure you don't split the stitches.

DESIGNER'S TIP

Go one step further and customize your bag (see left) with rows of running stitch worked in a chunky, tonal yarn. Here horizontal and vertical lines of running stitch have been worked to form a grid effect.

WORKING THE RUNNING STITCH

This simple stitch forms a decorative broken line.

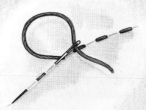

• *Working from right to left, bring the needle out to the front at your starting point. Pass the needle in and out of the fabric along the stitching line. Work several stitches at a time, keeping the length and tension even.*

• *For a solid line, work a double running stitch. Work a row of evenly spaced running stitches along the stitching lines. Turn the work around. Work another set of running stitches, filling the spaces left by the first stitches and using the same holes.*

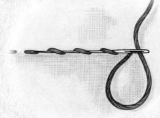

• *To secure the thread end when you have finished, push the needle to the back of the fabric. Weave the thread into the back of several stitches and trim the tail.*

BEANIE

Pull on this snug beanie to keep hair under control—or to cover it up if you have to run out. It is knitted in the mock English rib, a stitch that ensures plenty of stretch.

MATERIALS

- 4 x 1 oz. (25g) balls of Crea Impasto in Pebble
- Pair of size 6 (4.0mm) knitting needles
- 6 stitch markers
- Tapestry needle

Go to Knitting Basics pages 82–94 for advice on stitches, problem solving, and finishing your knits.

DESIGNER'S TIP

If you don't have special markers for your knitting, you can use loops of yarn instead. Choose a yarn in a contrasting color so that the markers are visible on the needle.

SIZE

To fit 21¼ in. (54cm) head circumference. Length: 7 in. (18cm), with the brim rolled back.

GAUGE

23 sts and 30 rows = 4 in. (10cm) over st st.

ABBREVIATIONS

See back flap.

SPECIAL ABBREVIATION

Ssk = slip, slip knit worked as follows: sl the next 2 sts k-wise, insert the left needle into the 2 slipped sts, from left to right, and k them tog.

TO MAKE

Using size 6 (4.0mm) needles, cast on 119 sts.
Beg with a k row, work 10 rows st st for the brim, ending with a p row.
Work in the mock English rib patt as foll:
Row 1 (rs): K3, *p1, k3, rep from * to the end of the row.
Row 2: K1, p1, *k3, p1, rep from * to the last st, k1.
These 2 rows form the patt.
Rep them 13 more times.

Shape crown

Keeping the patt correct, shape as foll:
Dec row 1: Patt 9 sts, *place marker on the right needle, ssk, patt 17 sts, k2tog, place marker on the right needle, patt 19 sts, rep from * once more, place marker on the right needle, ssk, patt 17 sts, k2tog, place marker on the right needle, patt 9 sts. 113 sts.
Next row: Work in patt as set.
Dec row 2: Work to marker, *sl marker, ssk, work to 2 sts before marker, k2tog, sl marker, work to marker, rep from * once more, sl marker, ssk, work to 2 sts before marker, k2tog, sl marker, work to the end of the row. 107 sts.
Rep last 2 rows six more times, removing the markers on the last row. 71 sts.
Next row: Work in the patt as set.
Next row: Work 1 st, *place marker, ssk, patt 17 sts, k2tog, place marker, patt 3 sts, rep from * once more, place marker, ssk, patt 17 sts, k2tog, place marker, work 1 st. 65 sts.
Rep last 2 rows seven more times. Remove markers on the last row. 23 sts.
Next row: K1, *p2tog, k1, p2tog tbl, k3, rep from * once more, p2tog, k1, p2tog tbl, k1. 17sts.
Cut yarn leaving a long yarn tail. Thread the cut end through the rem sts, draw up tightly and secure the end.

FINISHING

Sew the back seam, reversing the seam for ¾ in. (2cm) on the brim (see Knitting Basics page 92).
Sew in the ends.

SHAWLETTE

Wrapped around your shoulders, this chic shawlette adds panache for any occasion. It is knitted in the stockinette stitch with a feminine rose spiral as a statement trim.

MATERIALS

- 6 x 1 oz. (25g) balls of Crea Grisaille in Fog
- 1 x 1 oz. (25g) ball of Crea Provenance in Granite
- Pair of size 8 (5.0mm) and size 6 (4.0mm) knitting needles
- Tapestry needle
- Brooch pin

SIZE

20⅛ in. (53cm) wide at center x 48 in. (122cm) long.

GAUGE

15 sts and 24 rows = 4 in. (10cm) over st st.

ABBREVIATIONS

See back flap.

TO MAKE

Using size 8 (5.0mm) needles and Fog, cast on 8 sts.
Row 1 (rs): K to the end of the row.
Row 2: K3, p2, k3.
Row 3: K2, inc in the next st, k to the end of the row. 9 sts.
Row 4: K3, p to last 3 sts, k3.
Rep the last 2 rows until there are 80 sts, ending with Row 4.

Next row: K3, k2tog tbl, k to the end of the row. 79 sts.
Next row: K3, p to last 3 sts, k3.
Rep these 2 rows until 8 sts rem, ending with a ws row. Bind off leaving a long yarn tail.

SPIRAL ROSE: Using size 6 (4.0mm) needles and Granite, cast on sts for the length required and make as in Steps 1 and 2 of the Design Bank on page 75. Starting at one end for the center, coil the strip to form a flower shape. Sew the short end and center in place, then sew a brooch pin to the back.

FINISHING

Weave in the yarn ends.
Add your own knitted flower brooch fastening.

EXPERT TIP

The loops in the bouclé yarn can make it difficult to see where to insert your needle for the next stitch. Take your time and make sure your stitches are not too tight.

The bouclé yarn makes the shawlette so warm, you'll want to wear it everywhere.

DESIGNER'S TIP

Customize your shawlette with three pom-poms in Albite (see Winter Walks Design Bank page 19) and using a 2⅛in. (5.5cm) diameter pom-pom maker. Then fasten it with a striking shawl pin, kilt pin, or brooch.

DESIGN BANK: **KNITTED SPIRALS**

Add designer panache to your projects by applying
knitted spirals. Leave them hanging or coil them
into pretty flowers as shown on the shawlette.

An unusual decorative trim adds unique character to a knitted project, taking it to a new design level—garments and items for the home, such as pillows and throws, can benefit from a three-dimensional decoration.

Narrow knitted spirals can be used to add a chunky fringe to the edges of garments and soft furnishings. Both wide and narrow spirals can be coiled to form flowers that make ideal decorations for a whole host of items.

KNITTED SPIRALS

To create a spiral, the bound-off edge must be at least three times longer than the cast-on edge. The curl of the spiral appears as you bind off.

1 *Cast on the number of stitches you want depending on the desired length of the finished spiral. Work 3 rows in garter stitch. On the next row, knit twice into every stitch to double the number of stitches. Work 3 more rows in garter stitch.*

2 *On the next row, knit twice into every stitch to double the number of stitches again. Work another 3 rows in garter stitch. Bind off loosely. Weave in the cast-on tail and use the bind-off tail to attach the spiral to your project.*

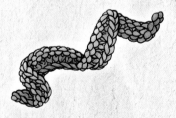

• *To make a narrow spiral, cast on the desired number of stitches to form the core of the spiral. Work twice into every stitch, then bind off loosely. For a slightly wider spiral, work 1 row between the increase and bind-off rows.*

PRETTY GLOVES

A pair of fingerless gloves is a practical choice for al fresco get-togethers. This pair is worked in the stockinette stitch with a simple lace flower border.

MATERIALS

- 1 x 2 oz. (50g) ball of Crea Harmony in Lilac
- Pair of size 3 (3.25mm) and size 4 (3.5mm) knitting needles
- Tapestry needle
- Yarn, crewel wool, or stranded embroidery floss in pale green

Go to Knitting Basics pages 82–94 for advice on stitches, problem solving. and finishing your knits.

EXPERT TIP

If you're new to knitting lace and are worried about keeping track of the pattern repeats, place a stitch marker at the end of each repeated section.

SIZES

8[8⅝:9½] in. (20[22:24]cm) in circumference x 5½[5½:6] in. (14[14:15]cm) long.

GAUGE

23 sts and 32 rows = 4 in. (10cm) over st st.

ABBREVIATIONS

See back flap.

TO MAKE

Using size 3 (3.25mm) needles cast on 46[50:54] sts.
Rib row 1 (rs): K2, *p2, k2, rep from * to the end of the row.
Rib row 2: P2, *k2, p2, rep from * to the end of the row.
Rep these 2 rows six more times, but inc 0[1:2] sts evenly on the last row. 46[51:56] sts.
Change to size 4 (3.5mm) needles.
Beg with a k row, cont in st st until work measures 4⅜[4⅜:4¾] in. (11[11:12]cm) from the beg, ending with a p row.
Now work the lace flower border as foll:
Row 1 (rs): K4[5:6], *k2tog, yfd, k1, yfd, skpo, k6[7:8], rep from * to the end of the row, finishing the last rep k4[5:6].
Row 2: P to the end of the row.
Row 3: K3[4:5], *k2tog, yfd, k3, yfd, skpo, k4[5:6], rep from * to the end of the row, finishing last rep k3[4:5].

Row 4: P to the end of the row.
Row 5: K5[6:7], *yfd, sl 1, k2tog, psso, yfd, k8[9:10], rep from * to the end of the row, finishing the last rep k5[6:7].
Row 6: P to the end of the row.
Beg with a k row, work 3 rows st st, ending with a k row.
Bind off k-wise leaving a long yarn tail.

FINISHING

Weave in the yarn ends. Fold the glove in half, with the right sides together, pin the seam leaving an opening for the thumb (see Knitting Basics page 92). Try on the glove and adjust the opening if necessary. Join the seam.
Work some simple running stitches (see Café Dining Design Bank page 69) in pale green along the sides of the central lace flower motif.
Make another glove in the same way.

Chilly hands will be a thing of the past with these beautiful fingerless gloves.

WATERFALL CARDIGAN

This cozy loose-fitting cardigan has casual cascading fronts that form a clever waterfall effect. It is knitted in the stockinette stitch with neat moss stitch borders.

MATERIALS

- 20[22:25] x 1 oz. (25g) balls of Crea Impasto in Pebble
- Pair of size 6 (4.0mm) knitting needles
- Tapestry needle

SIZES

To suit bust 34–36[36–38:38–40] in. (86-91[91-97:97-102]cm).
Length 19½[20½:21¼] in. (50[52:54]cm).
Sleeve seam 7 in. (18cm).

GAUGE

21 sts and 28 rows = 4 in. (10cm) over st st.

ABBREVIATIONS

See back flap.

TO MAKE

BACK: Using size 6 (4.0mm) needles, cast on 93[101:109] sts.

S st row: P1, *k1, p1, rep from * to the end of the row.
Rep this row 6 more times.
Beg with a k row, cont in st st until work measures 12 in. (30cm) from the beg, ending with a p row.

Shape armholes

Bind off 5 sts at the beg of the next 2 rows. Dec 1 st at each end of the next and every foll alt row until 73[81:87] sts rem.
Cont without shaping until the armholes measure 8[8⅝:9½] in. (20[22:24]cm) from the beg, ending with a p row.

Let the excess fabric fall naturally into shape for an effortless and classy look.

DESIGNER'S TIP

You can wear the flattering waterfall front open or secure the edges of the cardigan with a brooch.

Shape shoulders

Bind off 7[7:8] sts at the beg of the next 2 rows and 5[6:6] sts at the beg of the foll 4 rows. Bind off the rem 39[43:47] sts leaving a long yarn tail.

LEFT FRONT: Using size 6 (4.0mm) needles, cast on 115[125:137] sts.

Work s st row as given for the back 7 times.

Now work in st st with s st border as foll:

Row 1 (rs): K to the last 5 sts, p1, (k1, p1) twice.

Row 2: P1, (k1, p1) twice, p to the end of the row.

These 2 rows form the patt.

**Cont in patt until work measures 12 in. (30cm) from the beg, ending with a ws row. (For the right front, work 1 more row here.)

Shape armhole

Cont in the patt, bind off 5 sts at the beg of the next row. Dec 1 st at the armhole edge on every foll alt row until 105[115:126] sts rem. Cont without shaping until the armhole measures

8[8⅝:9½] in. (20[22:24]cm) from the beg, ending at the armhole edge.

Shape shoulder

Bind off 7[7:8] sts at the beg of the next row and 5[6:6] sts at the beg of the foll 2 alt rows.

Bind off the rem 88[96:106] sts leaving a long yarn tail.

RIGHT FRONT: Using size 6 (4.0mm) needles, cast on 115[125:137] sts.

Work s st row as given for the back 7 times.

Now work in st st with s st border as foll:

Row 1 (rs): P1, (k1, p1) twice, k to the end of the row.

Row 2: P to the last 5 sts, (p1, k1) twice, p1.

These 2 rows form the patt.

Complete as given for left front from **, noting the bracketed exceptions.

SLEEVES: Using size 6 (4.0mm) needles, cast on 61[69:77] sts. Work s st row as given for the back 7 times.

Beg with a k row, cont in st st but inc 1 st at each end of the 7th and every foll 8th row until there are 71[79:87] sts.

Cont without shaping until the work measures 7 in. (18cm) from the beg, ending with a p row.

Shape top

Bind off 5 sts at the beg of the next 2 rows. Dec 1 st at each end of the next and every foll alt row to 35[39:43] sts.

Bind off 3[4:4] sts at the beg of the next 2 rows and 3 sts at the beg of the foll 4 rows. Bind off the rem 17[19:23] sts.

FINISHING

Block the pieces using the spray method (see Knitting Basics page 94). Join the shoulder seams (see Knitting Basics page 92). Set in the sleeves, then join the side and sleeve seams.

The seed stitch borders create a neat finish to the edges and cuffs.

EXPERT TIP

Take time when you block the cardigan and make sure that the edges are straight. This will give the garment a professional finish and enhance its structure and drape.

KNITTING BASICS

CASTING ON

By following these simple steps you can learn how to cast on with two needles, work knit and purl stitches and bind off—the basic techniques you need to start knitting.

SLIP KNOT LOOP

Begin by making a slip knot loop about 4¾ in. (12cm) from the end of the yarn. Place it on one knitting needle—this will count as the first stitch.

TWO NEEDLE CABLE CAST ON

This is an attractive all-purpose cast on with a neat, firm edge. It has a certain amount of "give" but won't stretch out of shape.

1 *Place a slip knot loop onto the left needle to create the first stitch. Insert the right needle through this stitch, from front to back. Take the yarn around the right needle.*

2 *Bring the yarn through the first stitch so that it forms a loop on the right needle.*

3 *Take the new loop from the right needle and place it on the left needle to make the second stitch.*

4 *Insert the right needle between the two stitches. Wrap the yarn around again, pull the loop through, and place it on the left needle as before.*

5 *Repeat to create as many stitches as you need, keeping the loops as even as possible. For a neat edge, keep the cast on gauge relaxed and even. This prevents the cast on edge from becoming too tight, making it easy to knit the first row smoothly.*

KNIT STITCH

By working every row in the knit stitch, you create a garter stitch fabric.

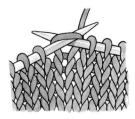

1 *Hold the needle with the stitches in your left hand. Insert the right needle into the first stitch, from front to back.*

2 *With the yarn in your right hand, use your forefinger to take the yarn around the right needle and up between the needles.*

3 *With the right needle, draw the yarn through the stitch, then slip the stitch off the left needle to complete the knit stitch. Repeat to the end of the row; turn the knitting ready to work the next row.*

BINDING OFF

PURL STITCH

Alternate rows of knit and purl stitch to create a stockinette stitch fabric.

1 *Hold the needle with the stitches in your left hand. Insert the right needle into the first stitch, from back to front.*

2 *With the yarn in your right hand, use your forefinger to take the yarn around the right needle, and down between the needles.*

3 *With the right needle, draw the yarn through the stitch, then slip the stitch off the left needle to complete the purl stitch. Repeat to the end of the row; turn the knitting ready to work the next row.*

BINDING OFF

When you bind off, it is important to maintain an even gauge.

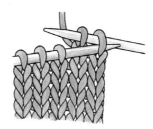

1 *Knit the first 2 stitches, then insert the point of the left needle into the first stitch, from left to right.*

2 *Use the left needle to lift the first stitch over the second stitch and off the needle to bind off one stitch.*

3 *Knit the next stitch, then repeat step 2 to bind off another stitch. Repeat until one stitch remains on the right needle. Cut the yarn leaving a 4¾ in. (12cm) tail and draw the end through the last stitch. Pull up to secure.*

GAUGE SQUARE

Before you start a knitting pattern, you should always work a gauge square!

WHY WORK A GAUGE SQUARE?

A gauge square is necessary so you can check that the size needles recommended in a pattern will give you the correct finished size; different people work in different ways and some hold the yarn more tightly or loosely than others—this will have a bearing on the finished size of the work. The gauge gives you the number of stitches and rows you must work, using the recommended yarn and needles, to obtain a 4 in. (10cm) square. If your gauge is not 4 in. (10cm) square, your project will be either too big or too small if you continue with the needles recommended in the pattern.

HOW DO I WORK A GAUGE SQUARE?

Using the stitch indicated, work a square at least 6 in. (15cm) with the size needles specified, then bind off. If the type of yarn permits pressing, press the square carefully. Stretch it very gently widthways if it has been worked in a rib pattern. Using a ruler, measure and count the stitches over 4 in. (10cm) across the width and the rows over 4 in. (10cm) along the length. Compare the results with the figures in the "gauge" section on your pattern.

I HAVE MORE STITCHES AND MORE ROWS

This means you are working too tightly. Work another gauge square using larger needles.

I HAVE TOO FEW STITCHES AND ROWS

This means you are working too loosely. Work another gauge square using smaller needles.

INCREASING A STITCH

Increasing is the technique used to enlarge the width of knitting. Increases can be made at the beginning or the end of a row, or several increases can be distributed across a row.

INCREASING ONE STITCH

The simplest way of increasing, making two stitches from one stitch, can be worked anywhere in a row. It is a convenient way to shape side edges, and it gives a gathered effect when you increase into every stitch.

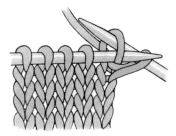

1 *To make two stitches from one, knit or purl into the stitch as usual, keeping the stitch on the left needle. Insert the right needle into the back of the same stitch and knit or purl the stitch again.*

EXPERT'S TIP

To work an invisible increase on a purl row, use the left needle to pick up the thread between the stitches, from front to back, then purl into the back of it. This increase is abbreviated as pup.

INVISIBLE INCREASE

This increase is made between stitches.

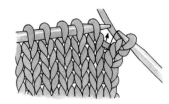

1 *At the beginning of a knit row, knit the first stitch, then insert the right needle under the thread between the stitch on the right needle and the first stitch on the left needle and slide the loop onto the left needle.*

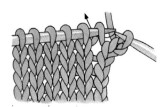

2 *Now knit this loop through the back to twist it. This avoids making a hole at the base of the new stitch. Continue knitting the row. This increase is abbreviated as puk.*

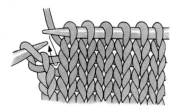

3 *At the end of a knit row, pick up and knit into the back of the thread between the stitch on the right needle and the last stitch on the left needle.*

INCREASING A STITCH SEVERAL STITCHES FROM THE EDGE

This increase is worked by picking up and knitting into a stitch one row below.

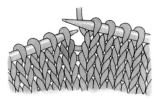

1 *Insert the right needle in the stitch just below the next stitch on the left needle (shown in a contrasting color) and knit one stitch, making a stitch on the right needle.*

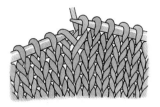

2 *Then knit the stitch on the left needle, making two stitches from one stitch.*

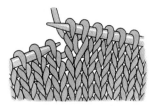

3 *You will now have one more stitch on the right needle. Work the increase at the end of the row in the same way, making sure it is the same number of stitches from the edge.*

DECREASING A STITCH

Decreasing, as the name suggests, is the technique used to reduce the width of knitting. Decreases can be made at either end of the row or across the row.

KNITTING TWO STITCHES TOGETHER

This decrease is shown worked on the knit side of the work and two stitches from the edge. If decreasing on the purl side, purl the stitches together.

1 Knit the first 2 stitches. Insert the right needle in the second stitch on the left needle, then in the first stitch.

2 Wind the yarn around the right needle and knit the 2 stitches together.

3 By knitting 2 stitches together, there will be one stitch less. The stitches of this decrease slant to the right. This decrease is abbreviated as k2tog or p2tog on a purl row.

SLIP STITCH DECREASE

This decrease is always made on the right side of the work. Here it is shown worked two stitches from the edge.

1 Knit the first 2 stitches. Slip the next stitch by inserting the right needle knitwise, as if for a knit stitch, and slip it onto the right needle without knitting it, then knit the following stitch.

2 Insert the left needle into the slipped stitch and lift it over the stitch you have just knitted and off the needle.

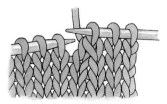

3 After a slip stitch decrease, there will be one less stitch. The stitches of this decrease will slant to the left. This decrease is abbreviated as skpo.

DECREASING ONE STITCH AT EACH END OF THE ROW

To form a neat diagonal line of shaping at each end of the knitting, two types of decreases are used on one row; skpo and k2tog. They are worked on the right side of the work at one or more stitches from the edge. This example shows the decreases worked one stitch from each edge.

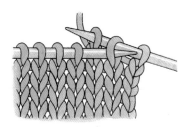

1 At the beginning of the row, knit the first stitch, then slip the next stitch and knit the following stitch. Insert the left needle into the slipped stitch and pass it over the knitted stitch. The decrease will slant to the left.

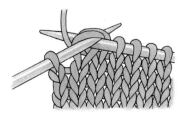

2 At the end of the row, when 3 stitches remain, knit 2 stitches together, then knit the last stitch. The decrease will slant to the right.

DROPPED STITCHES

Dropped stitches can happen to the most experienced knitter. Keep spare knitting needles, crochet hooks, and stitch holders handy so you can act quickly to rescue a stitch.

Locate the dropped stitch and stop it from unraveling further by holding it on a spare needle. If you drop a stitch as you work, simply pick it up and continue knitting.

A recently dropped stitch with its corresponding missed horizontal strand is easy to spot. You might even be aware of it happening as you knit and can pick it up immediately before you continue knitting the row.

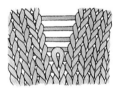

If a stitch has dropped down several rows, it appears at the bottom of a "ladder"— each horizontal strand is one row that it has missed. The stitch will need to be brought up the ladder, a row at a time, using a knitting needle or crochet hook.

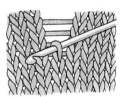

Once located, ease the rescued stitch gently onto a spare knitting needle, a crochet hook, or stitch holder to keep it stable. To pick up dropped stitches, you'll need a needle or crochet hook that is smaller than the ones you are currently using.

PICKING UP A STITCH FROM THE ROW BELOW

Hold the loose stitch on a spare needle, then work along the row until you reach the dropped stitch and pick it up as described below.

TO PICK UP A KNIT STITCH

1 *From the front of the work, insert the right needle into the dropped stitch. Then pick up the strand of yarn behind it so both are on the right needle.*

2 *Insert the left needle into the picked up stitch from back to front. Carefully lift it up and over the strand of yarn, keeping the new knit stitch on the right needle.*

3 *Transfer the rescued stitch to the left needle ready to continue knitting the row—make sure the stitch is not twisted.*

TO PICK UP A PURL STITCH

1 *With the wrong side of the work facing, insert the right needle into the dropped stitch from back to front, then pick up the strand of yarn in front of it so that both are on the right needle.*

2 *Insert the left needle into the picked up stitch and carefully lift it over the strand of yarn and off the needle, keeping the new purl stitch on the right needle.*

3 *Transfer the new purl stitch to the left needle ready to continue the purl row—make sure the stitch is not twisted.*

PICKING UP A DROPPED STITCH OVER SEVERAL ROWS

First, secure the dropped stitch and work along the row until you reach the ladder of unused strands. Work your way up the ladder to the top and then put the new stitch onto the left needle ready to continue the row.

Working up a knit ladder
Use a crochet hook that is smaller than your knitting needles. Insert the hook into the loose stitch from the front and catch the horizontal strand immediately behind. Pull the strand through the dropped stitch to create a new knit stitch. Hold this stitch on the hook and repeat to pick up the next rung of the ladder.

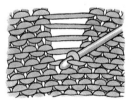

Working up a purl ladder
Insert the crochet hook into the loose stitch from the back and catch the horizontal strand in front of it. Pull the strand through the dropped stitch to create a new purl stitch. Remove the hook, bring the next horizontal strand in front of the new stitch, and repeat the process to pick up each spare strand in turn.

JOINING YARN

When you reach the end of a ball of yarn, or if you are working in stripes, you will need to join new yarn. Follow these simple steps to help you achieve a neat join.

1 *Insert the right needle into the first stitch as if to knit it, leave the yarn tail hanging.*

2 *Pick up the new ball of yarn and make a loop, leaving a 4–5 in. (10–13cm) tail to sew in—here a contrasting color has been used for clarity.*

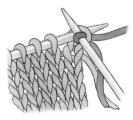

3 *Place the loop over the right needle and knit the first stitch.*

4 *Hold the tail of the old yarn and the new yarn in your left hand, then take the yarn from the new ball under and over these two ends of yarn to "secure" them.*

5 *Continue knitting with the new ball of yarn. When working in stripes, join a new color in the same way.*

EXPERT'S TIP

It can be frustrating to find you do not have enough yarn to complete a row. A row of knitting usually takes a length of yarn between two and a half and three times the width of the knitting, so make sure you have enough yarn before you start the row.

SIMPLE CABLES

Cables introduce intriguing surface patterns and texture to knitted fabrics. They vary from simple rope twists to multiple combinations that create complex and rhythmic 3D effects.

Cables are formed when groups of stitches change places at regular intervals. This creates the characteristic twisted effect of cabling. The number of stitches to be moved and the spacing between each twist can vary, and almost any weight of yarn can be used. The basic cabling technique produces an infinite variety of effects from subtle and delicate to bold and decisive, and can be used for anything from dainty baby garments to chunky pillows and throws.

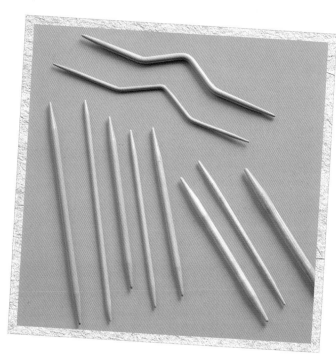

In order for the stitches to change place, a specified number must be kept aside ready to be picked up and knitted later. Small cable needles are used for this purpose, holding the stitches behind or in front of the knitting as required by the pattern. Cables are usually worked in stockinette stitch against a contrasting background of reverse stockinette stitch to display the cable pattern to full effect.

CABLE NEEDLES

Cable needles make light work of the cabling technique, so make them part of your knitting kit. They come in a variety of materials, sizes, and styles. Select the size and shape that is suitable for the pattern and yarn you are using and you find easiest to work with. For cables involving just a few stitches, a straight needle is fine. For cables involving a large number of stitches, and for thicker yarns, choose a needle with a pronounced bend or one that resembles a large hook that will prevent the stitches from slipping off. Choose a small, medium, or large needle that is slightly smaller than your knitting needle. And use an extra-large cable needle for cabling with very chunky yarns.

EXPERT'S TIP

Never try to work a cable using a normal long knitting needle or crochet hook. This will be very cumbersome to manipulate and is likely to cause dropped stitches and much frustration, making heavy work of an essentially simple technique.

WORKING A SIMPLE CABLE

Follow the instructions below for a basic 8-stitch cable worked against a reverse stockinette stitch background. You can make a narrower cable by using four or six stitches to create the pattern.

AN 8-STITCH CABLE TWISTING TO THE LEFT

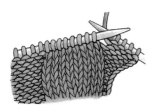

1 *In knitting patterns, a cable that twists to the left is abbreviated as C8F. Work a right-side row to the position of the cable.*

2 *Carefully slip the next four stitches onto a cable needle and hold them at the front of the work.*

3 *Keeping the four stitches on the cable needle at the front, knit the next four stitches on the left needle.*

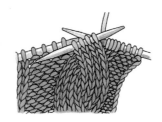

4 *Now carefully maneuver the cable needle so you can knit the four stitches held on it.*

5 *The eight stitches have now changed places and are all on the right needle. The cable maneuver is complete.*

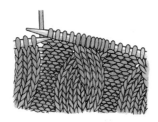

6 *Work in reverse stockinette stitch to the position of the next cable. In this sample there are four stitches between the cables, and the twists are worked on every tenth row, always with the right side facing.*

AN 8-STITCH CABLE TWISTING TO THE RIGHT

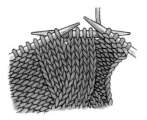

1 *In knitting patterns, a cable that twists to the right is abbreviated as C8B. Work a right-side row to the position of the cable. Slip the next four stitches onto a cable needle and hold it at the back of the work.*

2 *Knit the next four stitches on the left needle, then carefully knit the four stitches from the cable needle. The eight stitches have changed places and are now on the right needle creating a cable that slants to the right.*

EXPERT'S TIP

If you find it tricky to knit the stitches directly from the cable needle when completing the cable twist, simply return these reserved stitches back to your left needle and knit them as usual.

JOINING SEAMS

Once you have finished your knitting, the pieces will need assembling. Follow the steps where to achieve a professional finish—untidy seams can ruin a beautifully knitted project.

MATTRESS STITCH

This is worked on the right side of the knitting and makes it easy to see how your seam looks.

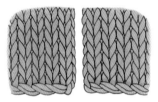

1 *Place the two pieces to be joined side by side, with the right side of the fabric facing you.*

2 *Thread a tapestry needle with matching yarn. To start the seam, insert the needle from back to front through the corner of the right piece, then through the corner of the left piece.*

3 *Make a figure-of-eight and insert the needle from back to front into the lower edge on the right piece, close to where you started. Pull the yarn through and pull up to join the two pieces.*

4 *Insert the needle under the horizontal bar between the first and second stitches on the left piece, then under the corresponding horizontal bar between the first and second stitches on the right piece. Continue to work between the pieces until a few rows have been worked.*

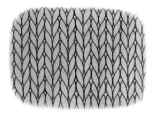

5 *Carefully draw up the yarn to close the gap—do not pull too tight or you'll distort the knitting. The seam will show on the wrong side and be invisible on the right side. Continue to join the seam in this way. Fasten off at the top by working a few small stitches on the wrong side.*

EXPERT'S TIP

You can also join stitches with the mattress stitch. Working on the right side, take the two vertical threads of a stitch on one side, then the two vertical threads of the corresponding stitch on the other side and pull up the yarn to draw them together. Continue in this way.

BACKSTITCH

The backstich creates a strong seam and can be used as an alternative to the mattress stitch, although it is not invisible.

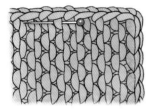

1 *Place the two pieces to be joined with the right sides together and the edges level. You can hold the pieces together, or insert a row of pins to hold them in place.*

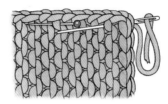

2 *Thread a tapestry needle with matching yarn and work a few small stitches on the edge of the back piece to secure the yarn. Working one stitch in from the edge, insert the needle from the back to the front one or two rows along—see Expert's Tip.*

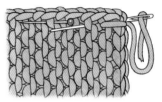

3 *Take the needle back over the rows and insert it close to the edge and pull the yarn through. Now insert the needle one or two rows along from the last stitch and pull the yarn through.*

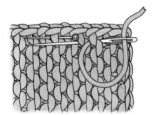

4 *Insert the needle at the point where the last stitch was worked, then bring it to the front one or two rows along.*

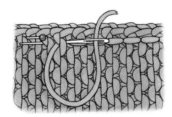

5 *Continue to work in this way, inserting the needle at the point where the last stitch was worked, then bringing it out to the front two rows along. Secure the yarn with a few small stitches at the end of the seam.*

EXPERT'S TIP

Work the backstitch over one or two rows, depending on the thickness of the yarn used for the project. For chunky yarns, work over one row; for finer yarns, work over two rows.

When joining stitches with the backstitch, stitch close to the edge and work over one or two stitches.

TACKING STITCH

It is sometimes necessary to tack pieces together before joining a seam. Work a few small stitches on the edge to secure the yarn. Working one stitch from the edge, insert the needle from back to front one or two rows along. Take the needle back over the rows and insert it close to the edge and pull the yarn through. Now insert the needle one or two rows from the last stitch and pull the yarn through. Take the needle over and then under the rows to form single stitches along the edge. Secure the yarn at the end with a few small stitches.

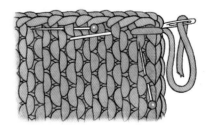

BLOCKING YOUR WORK

Blocking describes the method of stretching, shaping, and molding
a finished piece of knitting using heat, water, or steam.

WHY BLOCK FABRICS?

Blocking is an essential step that is sometimes overlooked. Blocking can:

- Give your work a neater and more professional finish as it relaxes the fibers and evens out your stitches.
- Increase the size of your work to the correct measurements (but it cannot make your work smaller).
- Mold your designs to a specific shape.
- "Open up" lacy designs to emphasize the stitches and patterns.
- Help curled edges lay flat.
- Improve the drape of your fabric.

EXPERT'S TIP

To block your knitting you need a flat, padded surface such as a purpose-made blocking board, interlocking foam pieces, an ironing board, or even carpet covered with plastic and a towel. To make your own blocking board, place a thick piece of wadding onto a rectangular board and cover them with a piece of checked fabric. Secure the fabric to the back of the board without distorting the checks as you will use these to line up your work.

SPRAY BLOCKING

Suitable for delicate and man-made fibers.

1 *Using rustproof glass-headed pins or blocking pins, pin out your pieces onto your blocking board to the dimensions specified in the pattern. Gently ease the fabric into place, making sure you do not distort the stitches and the edges are straight or curved as required.*

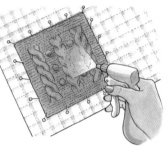

2 *Spray your work with cold water until it is damp but not saturated. Press gently with your hands to even out the fabric, then let dry completely before removing the pins.*

3 *If the desired result is not achieved, you can repeat this process again.*

STEAM BLOCKING

Suitable for some wool fibers and cottons.

1 *With the wrong side facing, pin out your pieces as for spray blocking.*

2 *Hold a hot iron or steamer close to the fabric and steam until it is damp. DO NOT place the iron or steamer directly onto the fabric because you will scorch the fibers.*

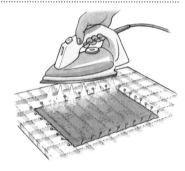

3 *If you need to press your work, place a clean colorfast cloth or towel over your fabric and press lightly at the temperature* recommended on the ball band. Once your work is completely dry, remove the pins.

WET BLOCKING

Suitable for most wools, silk, and other natural fibers.

1 *Fill a basin with cold or lukewarm water (check the ball band for temperature instructions). Immerse your fabric into the water to wet it.*

2 *Lift the fabric out of the water and at the same time very carefully squeeze out the excess water. DO NOT lift the whole piece out of* the water. When soaking wet, it will stretch. DO NOT wring or you will damage your fabric.

3 *Carefully lay your fabric on a towel and smooth it flat. Starting at one end, loosely roll up the towel and apply a little pressure to squeeze out the excess water.*

4 *Unroll the towel, then place your fabric onto a blocking board and pin into shape according to your pattern instructions, using rust-proof pins or blocking pins.*

INDEX

For abbreviations please see inside back flap.

ACKNOWLEDGEMENTS

HEAD OF CREA: Becky Davis
DESIGN MANAGER CREA: Caroline Grimshaw

DESIGNERS:
Creative Consultant and Designer: Lynne Watterson
Melanie Porter: Cozy Cowl and Striped Neck Warmer
Emma Wright: Skinny Scarf
Monica Russel: Boyfriend Cardigan
Luise Roberts: Beanie

All photography by Lizzie Orme except p4tr, 5tc and br, 13, 14, 17, 18, 21, 34-35, 41, 53, 54, 56-57, 71, 77 and 78 by: Laura Ashman
with styling by: Jo Rigg.
Book art direction and design: Caroline Grimshaw
Illustrations by: Coral Mula
Adaptation by: Creative Plus Publishing Ltd

Photo credits: Backgrounds: p1 and throughout Dejan Gospodarek/shutterstock.com; p2 left and throughout FabrikaSimf/shutterstock.com; p4 and throughout schankz/shutterstock.com; p36 and throughout Lamyai/shutterstock.com; p58 and throughout arigato/shutterstock.com; p82 and throughout Alena Ozerova/shutterstock.com; p84 and throughout Natali Zakharova/shutterstock.com. Textures: p1 and throughout Chavarin jantanabuppa/shutterstock.com; digieye/shutterstock.com.